Praise for
Monastery to Matrimony

"*Monastery to Matrimony* is a stunning memoir of young girl's dedication to a world within a convent. The heart-hurting knowledge that it was time to leave finds her after twenty years of service. These pages are peopled with friendships and a sweeping journey to love and marriage. This colorful story entails one woman's passion to make a difference."

—Stellasue Lee, Ph.D., author of
Crossing the Double Yellow Line and *firecracker RED*.

"Every man and woman at sometime in life wonders if they have taken the right path. This story of a young woman struggling to find herself is one we can all relate to. Written with humor and honesty, *Monastery to Matrimony* offers a unique solution in this true story of a girl dedicated to becoming a nun who finds herself thrust into a new world. Even men will laugh and root for this resourceful, dare we say, 'heroic' young woman."

—Mark H. Newhouse, author of *The Midnight Diet Club*

Monastery to Matrimony

A WOMAN'S JOURNEY

Mary Ann Weakley

BALBOA.
PRESS
A DIVISION OF HAY HOUSE

Balboa Press books may be ordered through booksellers or by contacting:

Balboa Press
A Division of Hay House
1663 Liberty Drive
Bloomington, IN 47403
www.balboapress.com
1 (877) 407-4847

Because of the dynamic nature of the Internet, any web addresses or links contained in this book may have changed since publication and may no longer be valid. The views expressed in this work are solely those of the author and do not necessarily reflect the views of the publisher, and the publisher hereby disclaims any responsibility for them.

The author of this book does not dispense medical advice or prescribe the use of any technique as a form of treatment for physical, emotional, or medical problems without the advice of a physician, either directly or indirectly. The intent of the author is only to offer information of a general nature to help you in your quest for emotional and spiritual well-being. In the event you use any of the information in this book for yourself, which is your constitutional right, the author and the publisher assume no responsibility for your actions.

Any people depicted in stock imagery provided by Thinkstock are models, and such images are being used for illustrative purposes only. Certain stock imagery © Thinkstock.

Printed in the United States of America.

ISBN: 978-1-4525-9596-2 (sc)
ISBN: 978-1-4525-9598-6 (hc)
ISBN: 978-1-4525-9597-9 (e)

Library of Congress Control Number: 2014906993

Balboa Press rev. date: 06/30/2014

Dedicated to all the women
who gave years of their lives in service
to the educational system of the Catholic Church.
To my contemporaries who chose to serve
in diverse ministries after years of dedication in religious life,
and to those women who remain faithful to their vow of Stability.

In loving memory of my late husband, Harold Weakley,
for his pride in me, his unconditional love,
and his support of my writing.

Acknowledgements

This book would never have come to fruition without the numerous people who offered encouragement, advice, and just plain interest in my life as a nun—why I entered the convent and why I left. Their curiosity prompted this writing journey.

I owe warm gratitude to my nun and former nun friends, who offered a reality check on what I wrote about our way of life: Sister Sheila McGrath, Sister Marilyn Ring, Joan Cook, Rosemary Kelly, Sheila Warner, Claire Davis, and Marie Therese Gass, author and editor.

I offer sincere thanks to my first readers who made the suggestions that kept me going, even though, clearly, my first attempts were poorly constructed: Judith Walter, and Laurie Michaud-Kay, my writing buddies, who stuck with me through the process. To Nona Bauer, classmate, friend, author, I thank you for encouraging me to keep writing and making me feel like I knew what I was doing, and for your tireless editing. Thanks, also, to Ginger Manley, Olive Mayger, and Susie Dunham. Thanks to Karen Aldridge, Director of Living Writers Collective, a powerhouse of creative writers, who showed interest in my story. Special thanks to the members of the Oxford, Florida writers group for their excellent critiques.

Gratitude to renowned poet Stellasue Lee, who took precious time to read and offer input and encouragement, and Karen Johnson, a friend and partner in my decorating business. Their input was invaluable. Thanks to Pam Young for reading the manuscript and who intuitively saw value in it. I thank best-selling Southern author, Lisa Patton, for being my cheerleader.

I thank the members of the Spring Hill, TN Library Women's Book Club, who kindly read early chapters and offered invaluable feedback as to public interest in a memoir of a nun's life.

Thank you to friends, too numerous to mention here, for continuing to ask, "How's your book coming? When can I read it? I want the first copy." How could I not take the project to fruition?

I met many people at random—in a store, at the pool, on a plane, a cross section of America, who were fascinated with my story and wanted to read it. They inspired me to persevere.

Special thanks to Stephanie Cornthwaite, my check-in-coordinator at Balboa Press, who patiently answered every question and helped me transition my manuscript into a published book. Equal praise is due all the staff at Balboa Press. Thanks to Marsha Butler, my Florida editor, for her valued expertise in preparing my manuscript.

I appreciate the contribution of archived materials from St. Mary Monastery, Nauvoo, IL, that assured accuracy regarding people, places, and dates.

Preface

Monastery to Matrimony, a Woman's Journey, is primarily about my life in the convent. Portions of the book, portraying times before and after, complete the story. What initially began as a capsule of convent life grew into a sharing of my personal spiritual journey, a journey that continues. I decided to tell my story in response to the questions asked when people learned I had been in a convent: "Why did you enter? Why at age seventeen? What was it like? Why did you leave after twenty years?" Answering those questions brought me to in-depth soul searching. Feelings then surfaced that needed to be put to rest.

In my writing, I have revisited and related memories significant to my path. Others may have different memories of the same times and situations. This book is written from my perspective and it is based on how my life was affected. With the exception of a couple of name alterations, the people and places are real. The dialogue is a representation of the scenes, if not always the exact words spoken. I relied on friends to jog my memory on some school and convent details as well as local historical happenings.

A portion of the proceeds from the sales of this book will be contributed to COPE, the Children of Pokot Education Fund, a Christian mission located in Tapadany, Pokot, Kenya, Africa. The COPE mission, which grew from a Bible

School taught in one small hut, is now a full-scale education system with over six hundred children. COPE was founded in 1997 by Barbara O'Donohue of Lincoln, IL, who continues to direct the mission. For further information on Barbara and the mission, visit the website, www.childrenofpokot.org

Foreword

Monastery to Matrimony, A Woman's Journey is the story of an extraordinary life journey by a strong and courageous woman. Mary Ann Weakley shares her thoughts, feelings, and doubts as she made a decision about a lifelong commitment at a very young age. Her story illuminates the process of making such decisions before adulthood. It provides a template for nurturing the attributes that are required to eventually reverse those decisions, when necessary. *Monastery to Matrimony* gives insight into both the decision to enter a convent and the even more difficult decision to leave the convent. What may be most valuable, however, is the opportunity to see what enabled Ms. Weakley to not only make that choice, but also to move beyond it to a contented and fulfilling new life.

Ms. Weakley takes the reader along on her spiritual, emotional, and intellectual search for her authentic self. The memoir is filled with lessons and insights that can serve as a guide to those of all ages and belief systems, who are searching for their spiritual truth or facing important life-altering decisions. Her strength, courage, and commitment to following her inner voice can serve as an example for all.

—Judith Walter, author of *Fleeing the Nest*

Chapter One – *The Naming*

≈

"Miss Mary Ann Cahill, you will henceforth be known as Sister Mary Magdalen of the Mother of God." Father Labonte's voice resounded down the expansive nave of Saints Peter and Paul Church, over the crowd, and up to the choir balcony filled with women wearing black and white.

My shoulders relaxed. I stepped down from the marble steps at the altar, careful not to trip on the unfamiliar floor-length robe I had donned only minutes earlier. My mind flashed back to my childhood and my favorite little nun-doll. I never imagined that one day I would look just like her.

Looking straight ahead as I approached the church pew, I could see my parents smiling—knowing the name made me happy. As custom dictated, I had submitted three choices, resigned to the fact that I might not receive any of them. Fear of being stuck with a name like Sister Cunegunda or Cresentia, or one of a litany of other saintly women buried deep in the archives of forgotten saints made me cringe. I winced at the thought of being called Sister Cunegunda forever. It could happen.

Returning to the front pew, I joined my three classmates waiting eagerly for their turn. One by one the scene repeated itself. Just as the celebration of the Mass ended, a triumphant organ recessional sounded—our cue to march down the aisle and out of the church. Every voice vibrated in song. The sun burst through tall, stained-glass windows like a symbol of God's blessing on his new, white-veiled brides. Had a white dove image of the Holy Spirit winged above us, it could have been a scene depicted in a spiritual painting. My heart swelled with emotion. Thinking it must be a sign confirming my decision to become a nun, I dismissed the concern that my choice might be an impulsive, short-lived adventure. The ceremony of receiving the habit—the clothing of a nun—marked the completion of nine months as a postulant, the first stage of my training. As a postulant, I wore a black blouse, knee-length skirt, and black opaque stockings.

Seeing my reflection in the mirror—the long black robe and white flowing veil, I liked the image—I looked like a real nun. I knew the clothes didn't automatically lift me to a higher level of holiness, but at least I looked holy. Not a strand of my mousey brown hair showed, and only a small square of my face, eyebrows to chin, could be seen. My blue eyes and Irish smile gave me away.

That June day in 1954 launched the beginning of an austere novice year—twelve months of additional training—considered to be the most challenging year of our formation to be an exemplary nun— sort of a spiritual boot camp. Acceptance for religious vows depends upon successful completion of the canonical year. Canon Law, the law of the church, required one year of strict seclusion from the outside world, meant to remove any distractions hindering a pursuit in contemplation of God. I would be tested, shaped, and molded as a piece of clay until a model religious nun was extruded.

During the ceremony, Linda, my best friend since third grade, had the same look of disbelief she'd had a year ago, when I first told her of my plans to enter a convent. After cheerleading, dating, going to movies, and athletic events together, she found it incredulous that

I would choose such a life. She told me how saddened she felt seeing tears on my father's face during the ceremony. She doubted they were tears of joy.

He looked dapper in his Sunday three-piece suit. My mother, in a new beige suit, wearing a wide-brimmed hat and matching gloves, sat beside him. Mom smiled at me as I came down the aisle. I could see a mixture of pride and sadness in her eyes. She no doubt felt this bridal ceremony didn't measure up to the one she had imagined for me. The stripping of my baptismal name must have hurt also. She had waited through the births of four sons to name her only daughter.

Traditionally, when nuns received their habit, they were given a saint's name—either masculine or feminine—chosen because of a special devotion to a saint or out of respect and admiration for a parent. As a postulant, I had admired Saint Mary Magdalen for her devotion and courage in committing to Jesus. I longed to grow in love and dedication to him with Mary Magdalen as my model.

I felt holier than ever on that joy-filled day, though, only a few years earlier, I could never have envisioned taking such a path. Putting on a nun's clothing and accepting a new name signified a new beginning, a lifetime of commitment.

Chapter Two – *Setting the Dominos*

≡

At the age of fourteen, long before my ceremonial clothing and naming day, I made a decision that set my life tumbling on a path, like a row of dominos, toward that day in June when I put on the habit of a nun. I chose to go to an all-girls boarding school for high school. To someone who, until third grade, attended a one-room country school, boarding school was an alien idea.

During the spring of my eighth-grade year, a girl from church told me of her plans to attend St. Mary's Academy, a Catholic girls' boarding school in Nauvoo, on the western border of Illinois. I found her excitement about going to St. Mary's contagious. She talked of the fun of going away to school and meeting kids from different places. I had never heard of Nauvoo, much less the boarding school, nor had it ever occurred to me to go anywhere other than Bement High School, where I would already know all the kids.

My curiosity prompted me to seek more information, like, do nuns teach there? Are there boys at the school? Though I was pretty sure of the answers, I had to ask. I mentioned the idea of a boarding school to my mother, never suggesting that I might be thinking about it. The prospect of going to high school in a new town far across the state became an exciting and adventurous idea. I did worry that sending

{ 5 }

me to a boarding school would be a major financial consideration for my parents—just seven years after our farm home and everything we owned had been destroyed.

In March 1942, a merciless tornado shattered everything in its path, including every single, upright stick of our modest country house. The funnel dropped down unannounced through the heavy rain and dark clouds. Mother screamed my name; I ran toward her as the windows clouded with black dirt. The ceiling cracked at the corner of the front bedroom where I played. In the aftermath, with rain still falling, she led me safely through a mangled mess of bricks, boards, live wires, and glass strewn across the yard. After making our way to the driveway, we found shelter in the remains of the barn until help arrived. By God's mercy, I escaped the flying debris without a scratch. She sheltered me with her body as we clung together. Mom suffered a broken clavicle, and cuts and bruises from the wreckage. The twister stripped the leaves from the hundred-year-old maple trees in the front yard. Our refrigerator lay on its side on the grass, still intact. A few dazed and naked chickens wandered the barnyard. Shards of furniture and bits and pieces of personal possessions littered the yard and pastures. A letter returned to my mother had landed miles away in a neighboring state. Except for the little rosary beads of my nun doll, found attached to a light pole, nothing of mine survived.

Many times over the years, I would wonder how I could have escaped harm from the tornado that day in March. *Did God have a plan for me?*

After the tornado tore away our home, we lived in a rented farmhouse and my father continued to farm the land. Eventually, my parents moved the family to Bement, a nearby small country town in central Illinois, similar to hundreds scattered across the plains of the Midwest dotting a grid of corn and beans.

The sudden idea of boarding school surprised them. They liked the prospect of the Catholic education, but they didn't like the thought of me going away from home. They both promised to consider the idea, even though two hundred miles across the state to Nauvoo seemed far from Bement. The $400 annual tuition, room and board had to be a consideration. Such a choice seemed extravagant when a public school stood just across the street from our home.

I waited weeks for their decision. After long discussions, they agreed to part with me for the sake of giving me a Catholic education, which they obviously valued more than I did. A new experience remained my sole motive. No doubt, the benefits of a *finishing school* played a big part in their decision too. I grew up a tomboy on the farm with my four older brothers, preferring to run barefoot outside to playing inside or helping Mom in the kitchen. If my parents waivered in their decision, Catholic education became my trump card, though I had yet to learn what it meant to get a Catholic education.

While I waited for their decision, I shared my plan with Linda and Sonya, my two best friends. I tried to explain the boarding school concept; they found it completely foreign. To be honest, it remained but a curiosity to me.

"What does that mean? You'd go to school there, instead of Bement? Where is it? Would you have to stay there all the time?" Linda bombarded me with questions, trying to understand. "Why do you want to go away from home? Your parents won't let you. Will you ever get home? What about Homecoming?"

Through the summer, I anticipated being back for big events, holiday vacations, and long weekends. Linda and Sonya practiced for cheerleading tryouts, and talked of new teachers and courses. I didn't expect, nor did I like, the growing feeling of being left out of the preparation for high school activities at home.

The bright spot for me became the planning of my new school wardrobe with Mom. We sat together on my little single bed cutting and sewing nametags on every piece of clothing—skirts, blouses, socks, sweaters, even linens. Required uniforms for school and for Sunday Mass should have made me suspicious of the adventure, but even that first sign of uniformity didn't dissuade me. Coordinating outfits was a fixation of mine; things had to match, but not to the point of wearing drab uniforms. Emotions swung from excitement to sadness for both of us as we talked of the days ahead. The planning confirmed my decision; turning back was not an option.

The new burgundy Packard my dad bought—an unnecessary extravagance according to my mother—had been loaded with new blue and white Samsonite suitcases and a foot locker. Linda came to say goodbye. Our lives were beginning a divergence we could not have foreseen.

Route 10, the two-lane road heading west across Illinois, unwound like a long gray ribbon passing field after field interrupted only by reduced speed limits through identical small country towns—replicas of Bement. Looking back from the rise of the bridge, as we crossed the Illinois River in Havana, I felt home and everything I had left behind disappearing. The river below wound like a chasm severing my connection to home. I sat in the back pondering my brave adventure. Mother tried to keep up a happy banter. Dad remained silent much of the trip.

After four hours, the Packard rounded the final curve into the small town of Nauvoo. A four-story, dark brick building loomed high above us on the right bank of the road. It looked ominous, like a correctional institution. My stomach churned. I relaxed at the sight of a sign directing us to turn left toward St. Mary's Academy. We pulled in front of a brilliant red brick structure, with St. Mary's Academy carved in stone above the double-door entry. Girls my age streamed in and out of the building.

The Academy campus looked grand. Towering golden trees shaded picnic benches in the yard.

Veins of sidewalks connected several buildings. It reminded me of a mini-college, both awesome and intimidating.

The commitment I made that day set in motion a future I could in no way have predicted. The tumbling domino dots were connecting to a new path.

Chapter Three – *First Commitment*

⁓⁓⁓

I jumped out of the Packard, straightened my blue corduroy skirt, buttoned the matching vest, gathered my little red shoulder bag, and joined my parents walking up the wide sidewalk toward the double-door entrance.

Inside the large foyer, we lined up with other parents and freshmen girls waiting for the principal, Sister Rose. A rotund nun wearing a long, black robe and flowing veil, stepped out of her office to greet us— her image filled the doorway. For a moment, when she moved toward me, I feared I was about to be smothered in her bountiful bosom. She took us into her office to formalize the enrollment. The scene looked incongruous—a small office filled with not only her presence, but a huge mahogany desk where she held court. My parents sat in two small chairs facing her. I stood. She had plump, rosy cheeks made even plumper when she smiled. Gold-framed round eyeglasses magnified crinkles around her eyes. Her smile was warm, but her authoritative stature gave me the feeling it would be best not to cross her.

After performing the obligatory show of welcome, she ushered us into the hall and dismissed us with a nod, a half smile, and a "You'll like St. Mary's, dear," indicating our time was up. She turned to my parents, "So nice to meet you. We'll take good care of her."

As she spoke, I could see her looking beyond us, reaching her hand to the parents of the next newcomer in line. The warmth and charm repeated with the next student. My parents, both more familiar with nuns, may have felt her graciousness genuine, but I reserved my opinion. I felt it best for me to make a practice of staying out of her way.

It's possible I misread the message. It could have been my lack of confidence, a leftover from my sixth grade teacher, Mrs. Golden. As the lone Catholic kid in my Bement class, I felt singled out for being Catholic. I understood the meaning of discrimination before I knew the word. Though I had permission to attend Mass before school on First Fridays, she never missed a chance to reprimand me for my tardiness. I learned to keep a low profile. As time would tell, I found it best to be scarce around Sister Rose also.

My first introduction to nuns dimmed my enthusiasm a shade as Sister Rose passed us off to a senior in charge of taking freshmen to the second-floor dorms. In North Dorm, brown, iron bunk beds stacked along the walls in front of the windows stifled natural light. Identical, almost thread bare, pale blue spreads covered each bed. Dark wood floors added to the gloominess of a room that could have fit the description of a European orphanage. Small, three-drawer wooden stands separated the beds. I could see a single iron bed tucked in one corner by the door, covered with a white bedspread. A white canvas-like curtain drawn around it hung on wooden poles. In spite of the meager surroundings, I felt an excitement and readiness to explore. I hadn't yet begun to miss my little room at home.

Sister Scholastica, a small, thin nun, flitted around the dorm smiling nervously trying to make us feel comfortable, though *she* looked anything but comfortable in her role of responsibility. With so little of her face showing, I couldn't decide her age. Her skin, though wrinkle-free, had a dry and pale look making her seem old. Like all the nuns, she wore a long black robe, black veil over a white band across the forehead. A pleated, white, saucer-shaped fabric hung under her chin and around her face. Sister Scholastica, as Prefect, had responsibility for all things related to freshmen in the dorm. She claimed the single bed in the corner with the white spread. I had never been quite so close to a real nun before, and *never* did I expect to sleep in the same room with one. Sleeping so close to a bunch of freshmen couldn't have been her favorite duty.

My parents hovered around me, in no hurry to leave. Mother helped me finish unpacking and settling into the dorm while Dad visited with other fathers in the campus yard. Eager to explore and meet my classmates, I was ready for my parents to go. The adventure had begun.

Mother's eyes glistened with a threat of tears. She hugged me, reluctant to let go. "Don't forget to write at least once a week." I promised. Dad squeezed me tight, concealing his tears as he climbed into his new Packard. I wondered if he had bought the new car to impress other parents and the staff, sending the message that he could afford a new car and send his daughter to the fine school. No doubt Mom suspected the same. They began the four-hour trip home without me. I choked back the lump in my throat and went to look for new friends and explore the school and campus.

Two weeks later, sadness gripped me; I suffered the painful ache of homesickness. Home felt a million miles away. With all my heart, I regretted hastening my parents' departure. I lay awake at nights picturing Mom in the kitchen, washing dishes without her helper. I envisioned Dad sitting in his rocking chair, smoking his evening cigar as he read the paper. I wondered if they felt a void. I wrote home faithfully as I had promised, sharing the details of my daily life. Phone calls from or to home were a luxury and discouraged except under serious conditions. The only available phone for our use was in a tiny room off the front hall of the school. It probably had once served as a broom closet; a small chair was squeezed in. A black, candlestick phone with the earpiece hung on the side, sat on the sill of a tiny window. If we received a call, we were notified to go to the phone room and wait for the connection.

I lived through the pain of homesickness by treasuring letters from Mom. I savored every tidbit she shared about happenings at home. Linda's letters kept me in touch with activities at school. I savored details of the sports and dating scene. My own school activities and classes gradually absorbed my attention weaning me from homesickness.

My country roots gave me an appreciation of nature. I loved the scenic Mississippi River winding below the hilltop school. Before the Catholic nuns settled there in 1854 to begin a school for girls, the beautiful little town had been a magnet for pioneering groups.

On walks to the river, my friends and I ventured into the preserved cabins and shops in the flat land along the river where Mormon missionaries told of the life of Joseph Smith and his followers. We were fascinated to learn that in the mid-1800s Nauvoo was the largest city in Illinois and called Commerce. A movement grew to make Commerce the State Capitol of Illinois, but eventually failed.

According to the missionaries, Smith had a vision that prompted him to change the name from Commerce to Nauvoo, a name of Hebrew origin meaning City Beautiful. The hilltop setting overlooking the Mississippi River must have inspired the name. The missionaries explained that Joseph Smith and his followers, who settled in Nauvoo to practice their lifestyle and religion, were catalysts for the rise and fall in Nauvoo's population.

Touring the small brick structures, we read historic markers explaining Mormon history. By 1833, stores once rustling with people stood empty. Joseph Smith had been murdered; his followers forced to exit Nauvoo leaving empty dwellings along the river flats. Headed west, they took few belongings. They left behind tools in their woodshops. The blacksmith's hammer fell silent on his anvil, lonely hand-hewn tables longed for dishes stacked in the kitchen cupboard.

Nauvoo's claim to fame when I arrived was a factory on the edge of the Academy campus where the locals made bleu cheese. The smell of the odiferous cheese sometimes drifted toward open dorm windows. A group from Europe known as French Icarians, introduced the vineyards and the production of wine. Their descendants still bottle varieties of the Old Nauvoo Brand at Baxter's Vineyard. Learning of the exodus of the Mormons, the Icarians saw Nauvoo as fertile ground for their communistic community. Their leader, Etienne Cabot from Dijon, France, envisioned a Utopian society that would attract many Europeans eager to escape hardships in their countries. Over the years, development funds dwindled, dissention grew between factions. Without a steady source of income, the community began to divide, causing yet another migration from Nauvoo and the dissolution of the once thriving idealistic Icarian Society in 1856. The rolling Mississippi River winding around the picturesque peninsula remained the constant in the evolution of life in the small Illinois village.

The scenic peninsula jutting from the edge of the State beckoned a third commune-type group to its banks in 1874. Five Catholic Benedictine nuns from a convent in Chicago established St. Mary's Academy, a school for young ladies.

Seventy-five years later, St. Mary's welcomed me as a freshman.

Chapter Four – *Academy Life*

——

*L*ike all students at St. Mary's, I led a simple, sheltered life. The classes taught by the nuns were challenging. The only legitimate excuse to miss class was an ailment serious enough to confine you to the infirmary in the care of Sister Bernarda, the school nurse. Outside of classes and studying, entertainment consisted of playing softball or basketball, walks to the river on a moonlit night, a Sunday movie in Nauvoo at the theatre on Main Street, picnics at the state park, and jitterbug dancing to the 78s playing on the lounge record player. Every Saturday night, we gathered in the lounge to watch the only TV on campus. Programming in the 1950s was so limited, only the *Hit Parade* with Snooky Lanson, a program featuring the top ten songs of the week, held our attention on Saturday nights.

Saturday mornings brought a domestic ritual that roused us from our beds. Sister Scholastica buzzed in and out and around us with her delicate steps, overseeing our weekly chores: dusting nightstands, cleaning out drawers, ironing, washing hair, polishing shoes, and on and on. All chores had to be inspected, approved, and checked off by Sister before we could leave the dorm floor. Radios in the dorm blared, "If I Knew You Were Comin' I'd've Baked a Cake," or if in a melancholy mood, Vaughn Monroe's "You're Breaking My Heart" touched us as we chatted and shared each other's lives on those Saturday mornings. Letters from home or boyfriends, distributed to our mailboxes mid-morning, dictated the mood.

On Saturday afternoon, we were allowed one hour to go into town. Our main destination was Kraus's, *the* Nauvoo restaurant where we ordered a *Chocolate Food,* the decadent specialty sundae. The recipe, concocted by one of the waitresses, became a popular tradition with all Academy girls.

Chocolate Food Recipe
In a soda glass, alternate layers of vanilla ice cream,
vanilla malted milk powder,
chocolate-fudge syrup and nuts.
Top with whipped cream.

As underclassmen, we weren't allowed to sit in a booth at Kraus's to enjoy our ice cream. At home, normally Linda, Sonya, and I sat in a booth and had an after-school coke at Hill's Café, where we lingered and played our favorite tunes on the jukebox, but at the Academy, only seniors could sit in a booth. They were allowed *town time* any day of the week. All other classes were allowed one-hour on Saturday and one day a week after school. Such strict rules were meant for the benefit of merchants, we guessed. Otherwise, Academy girls would have filled Kraus's booths every afternoon. Groups of giggly girls camping out in stores, buying little to nothing, and possibly disturbing their regular customers, would not have been appreciated. Classmates Maureen, Lindy, Mary Lou, and I would order our chocolate foods at the counter and walk back to school savoring every bite of the sundae. Chocolate foods and good starchy convent cooking contributed to the fifteen pounds I gained during freshmen year. My new clothes were shrinking.

Senior class student council members were assigned to monitor underclassmen behavior in town and report back to Sister Rose if we talked to boys or acted obnoxious in public. Sometimes we felt like delinquents out on good behavior. With the weight I gained, I wasn't getting a second look from the town boys anyway.

Every Sunday, the entire school attended Mass in the convent chapel. Dressed in our blue and white uniforms we marched like little French Madeleines two by two down the block to the chapel. I would grab my black mesh chapel veil, fold it into a triangle, secure it with bobby pins on my head, and run to get in line in the Academy front hall. Sister Rose supervised our behavior, ensuring total silence.

Though monitored, scheduled, and regimented every day, we developed life skills for homemaking, a love of learning, critical thinking skills, opportunities for leadership, social graces, and understanding relationships. We learned tolerance of personalities, different backgrounds, and points-of-view. The nuns who taught us were our big sisters, our mentors and advisors. I never regretted making the decision to be educated by those self-sacrificing, dedicated women.

Sister Joann, a business teacher, soft spoken, but firm became a favorite of everyone. She had a sincere, warm smile and dark knowing eyes that could look right into you; no use trying to hide anything from her. I recall returning to school after one holiday feeling left out of the activities back home. I played a melancholy song on the record player, singing to it over and over, nostalgic for the fun of dating while home. Sister Joann, in her concern, pulled me aside and questioned my mood, "Are you all right? Did everything go all right at home?"

Students saw her as a patient listener and mentor, willing to give her undivided attention in the midst of dormitory confusion. We could always find her seated in her comfy chair in the corner of the second floor dorm at St. Joe Hall, where she prefected sophomores each evening after study hall. She would either read her breviary— book of prayers—listen patiently to the girls who sought her counsel, or talk about the Chicago Cubs. A sports enthusiast, she also coached our basketball and softball teams.

My basketball buddy, Lindy and I perfected our playing skills under Sister Joann's tutelage. Lindy came from New Mexico. Lanky Lindy of Mexican-Indian descent had deep, dark eyes that matched her raven hair. Her strong, hereditary Indian nose punctuated her naturally tanned skin and mysteriously somber face. She came to St. Mary's in seventh grade when her older sister, Susan, entered high school. Lindy and I were friends all through school and after, though we looked like an unlikely duo. I had fair Irish coloring, even temperament, and a consistent jolly mood. Lindy, on the other hand, was dark, with a solemn, moody look. Her perpetual scowl effectively kept people at a distance, lest they pry too deeply. I didn't pry, but I didn't keep my distance either. We developed a bond over our four years at the Academy.

As senior year approached, I began to think about what career I might consider and what college I would choose. Most young women in the 1940s and early 1950s were not aspiring to a career in the corporate world, and at that time, *entrepreneur* wasn't in my vocabulary. Teaching and nursing were the accepted career paths for young women who went to college. Since I had no desire to teach or to be a nurse, my plan was to get an associate degree and train for the business world as a secretary or administrative assistant. Never would I have aspired to the level of a vice president or president of a company. During one summer vacation at home, Linda and I investigated what we saw as a romantic career as airline stewardesses. When we discovered we wouldn't qualify under the strict height and vision requirements, we gave up that adventure. Her height and my need for corrective eye glasses disqualified us.

In seventh grade, one of my fantasies had been to sing like Deanna Durbin, and dance like Ann Miller. Linda and I had seen every one of their movies at the Bement Theatre. I did inherit Mom's vocal ability and might have done more with music if I had followed her sage advice to take piano lessons from Miss Rose, the serious-faced composer-musician, who lived next door to us. I balked at taking lessons from her because of her strictness, plus her house was dark and scary.

Without the rudiments of training, I lacked confidence in my musical ability, but singing would always be my companion, though it sometimes got me into trouble.

In Algebra II class, my singing brought me under the suspicion from Sister Camilla, our no-nonsense teacher.

"Who has that radio?" she asked before class one day.

She seemed to speak without moving her pencil-thin lips; a smile seldom crossed her face during class. Her ashen, chiseled features commanded discipline, and we obliged. I had been singing to myself before we settled down to business in class.

Everyone looked around the room. She insisted someone had a radio and focused on me. Looking red faced and guilty, I tried to assure her I had no radio. I had been singing.

"I know a radio when I hear it," she challenged, standing by my desk. My classmates weren't brave enough to come to my rescue, so I took the verbal reprimand and we all laughed later.

Sister Camilla's sternness betrayed the sweet, kind human being I later came to know. She wanted all of our attention on math. I remained especially grateful to her for sparing me from a report to Sister Rose, whom I continued to fear.

Chapter Five – *Sister Rose*

⸺

*T*he daily morning school bell echoed through the building, calling all students to morning assembly. One hundred and twenty girls in brown-on-brown uniforms scrambled from all directions to the lounge off the main hallway across from Sister Rose's office. We stood, row by row, the length of the green and brown block-pattern linoleum floor, waiting for morning announcements.

A hush fell over the room as Sister Rose took her place at the front of the room, standing with her hands tucked in the long, black leather strap of a belt around her girth. We stood silently frozen-in-place waiting for her to pronounce the directives of the day. Like little soldiers waiting for roll call, we stood lined up in four rows by class and by alphabet. We would sound off our names to verify our existence— Anderson, Banks, Bartlett, Cahill, Cain. An absence could hardly be expected since we all lived there.

Her announcements often ended with a list of girls she wanted to see in her office. If your name was on that list, it almost guaranteed you were in trouble. I always feared being the next target to draw her ire. It's hard to tell why I felt that way, because I always walked a straight and narrow path. I was hardly a magnet for trouble. Maybe it was a throwback to Mrs. Golden's class, though I shouldn't blame her for my paranoia.

Sister Rose monitored our freshmen religion class once a week. I say monitored because she didn't teach, she only tested us on memorization of the catechism, the instructional Q & A book on Catholic doctrine. She sat at her desk on a raised platform in the front. We lined up along the walls of the classroom. Looking down at us, she would read a catechism question to each in turn. If we answered correctly, we could sit down, as in a reverse spelldown. If not, we remained standing against the wall until our turn came again. I prayed for a short and easy question, like: *Who made you?*

Memorization was not my strength. Invariably, I would be one of the last ones standing. In my defense, I had never even seen a catechism before I went to the Academy. Many of the girls had memorized the catechism from first grade in their hometown Catholic grade schools.

I hated those religion classes. They made me feel less than Catholic, though I knew I must be a good Catholic because of all the training I had received at home. During Lent, we recited the rosary on our knees as a family. I attended Mass every Sunday, Holy Day, and First Friday with never a complaint. Those pieties had to count for something. I thought that made me a good Catholic girl.

I wasn't alone in my fear of Sister Rose. Many students would attempt to fade into the hallway lockers as she came lumbering out of her office, pounding the miniature black and white hall tiles with every step. Even the nuns on the faculty seemed scarce when Sister Rose came out of her office on a rampage.

She seldom just sauntered into the lounge to chat with students. With arms swinging, gold-rimmed binocular glasses focused straight ahead, she would leave her office heading for the bulletin board in the central hall to post the latest misdemeanor list. The expression on her flushed face was easy to read. One could only imagine what prompted the anger welling up from inside.

Her fist gripped the yellow, legal-size pages. The handwritten notice in her two-inch script was characteristic of her large and powerful presence. The size of the script, dwarfed only by her even larger signature, indicated the measure of her anger. One by one, we would creep out to read the proclamation, fearful of finding our own names listed.

I remember one particular incident when our class became the subject of the yellow sheets. An all-school basketball tournament invited each class to choose a distinguishing logo, colors, and name. In the costume closet, our creative sophomore class found black gym suits worn by St. Mary's girls in the 1920s. We found the long, bloomer-type legs hilarious. We decided they would give everyone a laugh and set us apart from other classes wearing the regular blue, tailored gym suits. We sewed for hours after school, Saturday and Sunday to get the suits ready for our debut in the tournament.

Word got back to Sister Rose about the Sunday sewing circle in the dorm. No laborious tasks were allowed on Sunday, a day of worship. We didn't consider sewing for our school event to be a laborious task. We were having fun.

The yellow sheets went up announcing the transgression. Our names were listed large enough to read three feet away. Our disrespect of the Lord's Day had enraged Sister Rose. Town privileges were taken away. In effect, we were campused. The dorm would normally have been locked on Sunday afternoon, but Sister Joann opened it for us to finish sewing in time for the tournament later that day. She, no doubt, felt Rose's wrath as well. It's a silly memory that has been recounted at every class reunion since. We may not have won the tournament, but we made the grandest entrance.

As ominous as Sister Rose could be, a soft, teddy-bear-like person showed up occasionally. That flip side of her personality was evidenced on those rare occasions when, after an evening study hour, she would announce on the PA, "Ice cream for everyone in the Sugar Bowl." Like ants in search of sugar, girls from every dorm beat a path to the

Sugar Bowl, the small restaurant-like store with soda-fountain style red tables and chairs in the low-ceiling basement of Mary Hall dorm.

The three-story Mary Hall building was the first convent of the sisters when they came to Nauvoo. Prior to that, the structure contained the ammunition arsenal for the Mormon militia, hence the three-foot-thick walls.

"Free ice cream bars or Dixie cups, compliments of Sister Rose," announced Sister Dolores, the Sugar Bowl store manager, and Rose's best friend among the sisters. The treat sometimes followed a successful sports tournament, grueling semester exams, or sometimes for no apparent reason at all. Sister Rose simply may have had a good day. Whatever prompted it, the impulsive gesture gave her "points." Years later I was privy to an analysis of her handwriting, bearing out that *generosity was not a strong trait—impulsive giving perhaps—but probably not genuine generosity.*

Many girls had a domestic job, a board job, which helped defray the full cost of tuition. Marian, one of my classmates, had the job of cleaning the front stairs near the entrance to the school. The proximity of the stairs to Sister Rose's office became Marian's downfall. Sister Rose used the stairs regularly since her bedroom suite opened just at the top of the second flight. Marian could never clean those stairs to Sister Rose's satisfaction. They were either too dusty or not polished enough. Marian would always smile and clean them, again and again. Looking back, I wondered if her decision to enter the convent after freshmen year was an attempt to escape those stairs and Sister Rose. I could think of no other reason she would become a nun at fourteen.

As I later learned, entering the convent could never be a path of escape from anything, especially Sister Rose.

Chapter Six – *Decision*

⸺

*T*hrough my years of high school I grew to admire those nurturing women in black robes. They inspired and encouraged us to reach beyond our grasp in all areas of life. In the four years I lived with them, I saw happy, fulfilled women dedicated to God and living in service to him through a mission to teach. I saw normal people who laughed and joked; no longer as mysterious as I once thought. Sister Rose ran a tight ship, but in the day-to-day encounters with our teachers and prefects we developed long-lasting friendships.

As graduation drew near, I was beginning to wonder if I should consider entering the convent. It crossed my mind that I may have been saved from the tornado to give my life to God. On the other hand, I enjoyed my life too much to make such a sacrifice. There was a struggle in my soul. The conflicting goals of college and convent kept me awake nights and distracted me by day. Thoughts of becoming one of them crept into my heart. Midway through my senior year, the stress of making that decision took a toll on my health. I lost my appetite, and dropped fifteen pounds of freshman baby fat. I was looking dramatically thin. If anorexia had been a cultural threat to one's health in those days, I would have been suspect.

Already away from home, family, and friends for the better part of four years, I pushed aside thoughts of becoming a nun. My parents wanted me to go to college, so I opted for that and made plans for the next fall. Once again, a search for something new and different attracted me to Barry College, a Catholic women's college in Miami. A cousin of mine went there. My pattern of choices was repeating itself. The University of Illinois, a short thirty miles from home, would have made more sense. Subconsciously, and later consciously, I think the Miami college plan became a subterfuge. It was unknown to most of my friends, a place I could talk about without showing a definite commitment to it. I could plan for Miami and reserve the possibility of entering the convent if I changed my mind.

Though eager to graduate and get on with my life, I felt a lingering sadness at the thought of leaving this peaceful place forever, never again to see these women who shaped me. I wondered if I was turning a deaf ear to God and dismissing his calling. I heard no distinct voice saying, "Come, follow me," nor did I receive a lighted vision showing me the way. If God spoke to me, it was through my recurring thoughts. But then, maybe that's the way he gives us messages. I couldn't honestly say God told me to go to the convent.

The college in Miami served as a convenient answer to the questions every senior is asked, "What are you going to do after graduation? Have you picked a college?"

I visited colleges in Dubuque and Davenport, Iowa, but never considered them. My talk of Florida was a way to procrastinate; it gave me time to think. I had not been dating seriously, so I was not influenced by a boyfriend. Marriage and family were never in my immediate plans. My thoughts always led me back to following in the footsteps of the nuns I admired.

A path less traveled had always appealed to me. My image of the life of a nun was tantamount to living a life in service to others. I hadn't considered how I would know his will. I began visiting the chapel often and praying for guidance, asking if I could lead this life that I knew little about. Religious education classes had improved my knowledge of Catholicism, but I wasn't sure I knew enough to be a nun. The question arose in my mind—*would they even want me?*

The reality of convent life didn't concern me. My total understanding of the life of a nun was based on what I saw in my teachers. They were happy, they loved their life, and they were dedicated to teaching. I envisioned myself as a bride of Christ. Wearing a long robe, flowing veil, and looking pious, was the romantic image of a seventeen-year-old. Never once did I consider that my vision of being a business teacher and a prefect at St. Joe Hall dormitory like Sister Joann might be a fantasy. My understanding of the vows of obedience, poverty, and chastity was superficial at best.

Sister Joann had frequently dropped hints suggesting I should think about entering her community. I developed an affinity toward her over the years, so it was natural for me to seek her counsel, asking if she thought I could be a nun. She knew me well and encouraged me to pray about it. I felt sure she thought of me as a good candidate. Not once did she challenge me as to my ability to live the life, nor did she ask if I had thought about giving up marriage and children. It would have been an obvious question for her to ask. I heard a rumor that she had been engaged before choosing the religious life. She must have pondered the choice of marriage and family versus convent. Being away from my family forever concerned me, but I had already been away for most of my teen years. I had not yet shared this idea with my parents or friends because I was still so uncertain. Sister Joann and all the sisters were careful not to give any clue to the rules or hardships of their life. From my perspective, I could see dedication, happiness, and peacefulness.

The month of March was always dedicated to discerning vocations. Displays and lectures on different walks of life—they weren't called careers—were exhibited, explained, and promoted. College recruiters visited the school. A nursing profession didn't appeal to me. The Peace Corps as an option for young people who wanted a life of service did not yet exist. If it had, I would have been first in line for that adventure and opportunity of service. Religious life displays depicted only one religious order—the Benedictines at St. Mary's. It never occurred to me there were a multitude of other religious orders also suited to my talents and interests. I was only interested in the Benedictine community.

Nearly every graduation class had at least two who would enter the convent. "Who do you think might enter from our class?" we often speculated in our dorm conversations. I kept my thoughts to myself, never admitting I was thinking about it.

The common path for high school girls was marriage, college, or working. Chosen careers led to nursing or teaching, and ultimately a husband. None of those options appealed to me at seventeen. Convent life seemed like an adventure—something totally different. Adventure suited my personality. I overlooked the fact that Nauvoo Benedictines were a teaching community and teaching as a nun is still teaching—the profession I didn't think I wanted. The adventure I could expect would be venturing into the unknown of convent life. I would not be traveling abroad to missions, nor did I want to. I just wanted something different from the usual path girls took after high school. College, work, marriage, children; it didn't suit me.

Though I had been struggling with the course my life would take, as with other decisions in my life, a point of clarity surfaced. In the weeks following graduation I stopped struggling. With my decision made, the vision ahead was becoming clear.

Chapter Seven – *Second Commitment*

≡

*I*n the summer of my eighteenth year, I was prepared to make the commitment to leave home a second time. Prepared may be the wrong word. Can any eighteen-year-old be prepared to take such a major life-changing course? Convents are forever, but at eighteen, my *forever* stretched only as far as my limited imagination. I could in no way visualize my future years—years of teaching primary grades, living with three or four older nuns in small-town convents, following strict rules and regulations bordering on archaic, never visiting family or sleeping in my own bed again. Maybe blurred vision of the future is God's gift to us so that we charge ahead into lifetime commitments with no fear or doubt, trusting him to guide us.

After all the discussions and plans for college, I worried what my parents would say about "changing horses in the middle of the stream," as my dad would say.

He sat in his rocking chair by the window in the dining room reading the evening paper, his after-dinner routine. Ashes grew on his half-burnt cigar without notice. After Mom and I finished the dishes, I asked her to join me as I mustered up the courage to interrupt Dad.

I had practiced many ways of breaking the news, but used none of the well thought-out phrases. "I think I want to enter the convent at

St. Mary's this fall," I said. The words echoed in my mind. I wondered if I really said them out loud. I looked down at the green checkered table cloth and fidgeted with the centerpiece bowl, turning it round and round. No one spoke.

Putting his cigar in the ashtray next to him just in time to catch the length of ashes, Dad looked up, crushing his paper in his lap. He looked at Mom for a sign that she had known and kept this announcement from him. She slumped into the closest chair at the dining room table—her hand went to her chest. They looked pensive, trying to deal with the sudden shift in my goals.

"Haven't you been in Nauvoo long enough? How long have you been thinking about this? Wouldn't you rather go to college at least for a year before deciding this?" My dad's first reaction was one of surprise and disappointment. He tried to hide it by chomping on his cigar.

Mother asked, "Have you thought this through? What about Miami? You were looking forward to college there. Why don't you think about this for a few weeks? Maybe go to college for a year, like your father says."

I agreed to think more about it and make up my mind later in the summer. After this brief discussion, Dad went back to hiding his feelings behind his newspaper while he pretended to read.

There were many questions in the next weeks, but despite the interrogations, they voiced no *major* objection to my choice of such a noble vocation. If I had come home and announced, "I want to get married this summer," Dad's first words would have been, "Forget it. Wait 'til you grow up," and the case would have been closed with no further discussion. Maybe it should have been their advice in this case. I was young and still infatuated with life at St. Mary's.

Young Catholic women were entering convents all the time— often right after high school. Parental acceptance is not *always* the case, but in general, Catholic parents were reluctant to interfere with a daughter or son's calling to a religious vocation considered a blessing to their family. There was no hope that any of my brothers would be priests. Bill had already been to the army and back, and was married with a wife and son. The other three showed no signs of considering the priesthood or even marriage yet.

Many Catholic mothers actually prayed for at least one of their children to be a priest or a nun, even encouraged them to seek that vocation. Knowing this, some young people felt they would disappoint their parents if they did *not* enter the convent. Mothers, in particular, felt blessed by God when their daughters or sons chose a religious life. They felt their place in heaven was assured. My being the only daughter gave them a different perspective.

Mother admitted she had suspected I might one day think about this choice. She always knew my mind before I did, but the timing caught her off guard.

"It makes me happy and it makes me sad," she confided. "I confess that years ago when I was your age, I considered becoming a nun." One of eight children, she too felt influenced by the lives of her high school nun teachers at St. Joseph's in Ivesdale. Meeting my father changed the course of her future. She became a wife and wonderful Catholic role model to her children.

I must have gotten my sense of humor and streak of independence and adventure from her. She told me tales of the fun she had as a young woman growing up in the small Catholic village of Ivesdale. There was mischief in her smiling eyes. As a teenager, she took a dare from her friends to drive the seven miles over dirt roads from Bement to Ivesdale, reaching Main Street before they could finish singing "Ninety-Nine Bottles of Beer on the Wall". She won the dare. No real bottles were involved. No wonder my father couldn't resist this fun-loving, risk-taking, and yet responsible young woman. She captured his Irish heart.

My final decision had come over time, sometimes with nudges from Sister Joann, suggesting that I *take the path less traveled*—her path. A prayer card she gave me once, struck a chord. The inscription read, *to whomsoever much is given, of her much is required.*

I had been given much in my short life. The boarding school days made me very aware of my blessed family background, a strong religious heritage, and a solid family structure. The years at the Academy awakened a new social awareness in me. I lived with girls who had no parents or close family ties. Their home situations were less than stellar. Often they had nowhere to go during holiday vacations—the Academy was their home. Some had been entrusted to the sisters' care from early childhood. The sisters substituted for their family. I wondered if maybe I should consider giving back.

Before I canceled the college application, I needed one more trip to the convent for confirmation of my decision. I needed to erase any doubt that lingered. I borrowed my brother Dick's Chrysler convertible, took Carole, a friend from the Academy, and drove to Nauvoo to meet with Sister Joann and Mother Ricarda, the superior. Cars are my weakness, especially convertibles. We put the top down just before reaching Nauvoo. Maybe I secretly hoped if they saw me looking materialistic and worldly in the flashy convertible, they would not consider me a good candidate. It didn't work. They concluded that if I was willing to give up such an alluring life, I could make the sacrifices necessary to be a good nun. There was that word, *sacrifices.* I wondered what and how many sacrifices were ahead of me.

By the end of the summer, I had canceled my registration at the college in Miami and planned for the final trip to Nauvoo, a trip of no return.

The wardrobe list this time was considerably different. No blue and white Samsonite luggage filled with colorful matching outfits. Black was the color of choice on the convent list.

Eileen, one of my Catholic girlfriends in Bement, volunteered to go shopping with me for nun shoes. We looked around the shoe department of Linn and Scruggs, a large department store in Decatur. Easing our way over to black and brown conservative looking shoes, trying to be inconspicuous, I picked up one and asked the clerk to see the pair in size seven, black.

"Are they for your grandmother?" the sales clerk asked as she showed me the pair.

"No, they're for me."

"Oh," her eyes darted away as I fitted them. I slipped my foot into the right shoe and laced it.

"Sorry, this is unreal. I can't help it." Eileen walked away, convulsed in giggles, as I tried on the old-lady, black-tie oxfords with square, chunky heels." My bobby sox didn't enhance the look. Long black stockings were next.

Eileen gave me no help with my resolve to complete the wardrobe list. Mom would have been right next to Eileen stifling her giggles, but she opted out of the shoe expedition and Linda just couldn't believe I was serious about the whole thing.

Mom bought me a beautiful place setting of sterling dinner ware, a list requirement—though sterling wasn't necessary. The silver pattern, lily of the valley, had been a favorite of mine since I learned she carried Lily-of-the-valley flowers in her wedding bouquet. Three of her good white satin brocaded napkins from her best linen set and a sterling silver napkin ring with my initials on it completed the refectory requirements.

I still have a photo of Linda and me taken in front of my Piatt Street house on that farewell summer day. Linda in her shorts, a sleeveless top and a long face, me in my church-going, aqua linen shirtdress and white linen heels.

"I can't believe you are leaving again, and this time for good," Linda said. "I thought your adventure flings were over after you came home from boarding school."

"I know, Lin. I didn't expect to be doing this either, but it is something I feel I must do. I am being pulled back there." We shared a long hug. The final photo of us could have originated the cliché, "looks like she lost her best friend." We both had.

The mood became melancholy on the two hundred-mile journey over the familiar road to Nauvoo. The finality of this trip weighed heavily on my mind. My father sought reassurances that my decision was final.

"You can still change your mind, you know." he interjected into the silence. Compared to the ride when I left as a freshman, this one had all the somberness of a wake. One last time, we drove around the final bend of the Mississippi River into the familiar little town of Nauvoo. We turned to the right at the top of the hill toward the dark brick building I once thought looked like a correctional institution—one block from the bright red academy building where it all started for me. One block in distance—centuries in time.

Dad parked the car on the gravel drive at the front door. We sat for a moment, looking for signs of life. I didn't expect a welcoming committee, but a familiar face would have been a comfort. An entrance sign on the door invited us in. With some trepidation, we stepped into the small, dark foyer and found a bell below a sign that read, *Ring for Service*. Shattering the silence, the tinny ring bounced in echoes through the empty halls. Hard to imagine there would be no one home—over 120 nuns lived there. Soon we heard quick footsteps and the swish of a long skirt rushing down the hall.

The novice mistress, in charge of all new members, greeted us with enthusiasm and warmth. "You must be Mr. and Mrs. Cahill, and Mary Ann. Welcome, dear. I am Sister Philomene."

The thin, wiry nun moved with nervous, jerking steps, like a mechanical doll with hinged limbs draped in yards of wool. She had a small face, square and pale, deprived of vitamin D.

She was "one of the Sloan girls" from an Irish family in Ivesdale. The familiar family name relieved my dad; he felt better knowing he would be leaving me with hometown folks. The empty, dark, narrow hall had a spooky silence. No other sisters were in sight. I had hoped maybe one or two of my teachers would be there to greet me.

Sister Philomene ushered us into a little parlor with three straight-back wooden chairs and a piano. It was a music room doubling as a greeting parlor. There were no voices in the background. The silence made us feel we should whisper. Sister Philomene brought us a soft drink and visited with us for a short time before my parents were encouraged to leave. Dad brought my sparse luggage into the stark entrance hallway where we were to say our goodbyes. Unlike at the Academy, Mom had no opportunity to help me unpack, to see where I would room, or to meet other sisters. It wasn't college. I wasn't moving into a girls dorm.

The first day they brought me to St. Mary's, I practically pushed my parents out the door. Exploring the campus was on my mind. This time I felt no desire to begin exploration of the dark and quiet building. I had never felt quite so unsure of my next move. Every fiber of my body felt freedom of choice might soon be taken away from me. I had come this far, I couldn't turn back now before I barely got in the door.

I tried not to show my ambivalent feelings when saying goodbye to my parents. I knew their final departure meant I would not be home for the next football homecoming, or Thanksgiving, or any other holiday, or home at all for any event. This big dark building was my home now. Sister Philomene assured them—and me—I would be well taken care of. Showing signs of skepticism, my father thanked her, gave me that tight hug with tears in his eyes. Solemn and brave, Mom kissed me goodbye. Leaving me there probably didn't feel much like a blessing from God. Once again, they made the turn-around trip back home without me. This time it was permanent. Sister Philomene put her arm around me as I cried for the pain I was selfishly causing in their hearts.

The small, dark green footlocker that took me to high school, moved into the convent with me. It held all of my personal clothing, black stockings, shoes, and the required towels and table napkins. For years to come, the footlocker would go with me from mission to mission. Materially, my personal possessions were reduced to the contents of a footlocker, a symbol and a reality of poverty.

The sentiment of bringing special things to remind me of home was a waste. After unpacking, neither the napkins, nor the silverware were seen again. In the spirit of poverty and community living, they went into general use. Sister Philomene spirited them away with the comment, "We'll put these away now." I took that to mean "put them away until mealtime." I misread that message. Only the initialed napkin ring reappeared later for my use. Since I didn't value the spirit of poverty and community living just yet, my first experience of detachment was hard to swallow—a first flaw in my vision of convent life. Had I known things I brought from home would be confiscated for general use, I could have spared my parents the expense of the fancy silverware, and my mother could have kept the good napkins with her set. What she meant to be a daily reminder of home became instead, a daily reminder that I had left home.

Personal items, such as records, radios, or cameras were not on the list. Those were considered superfluous—to them, not to me. It was the beginning of learning detachment from worldly goods.

Later, I found I was the only *oddball* to bring the nun-style black, oxford heeled shoes. The other postulants brought black loafers like any normal eighteen-year-old would wear. I always went a little overboard trying to do the right thing. I had to ask my mother to send me black loafers. The old-lady, oxford heels waited in my trunk for almost a year until I received the full long black habit, the dress of a proper nun. I then had the best-looking shoes of the group while the others wore plain convent issue.

Chapter Eight – *The Convent*

---

*L*indy, my roommate at the Academy, and I never talked of our plans to enter the convent. I chose to struggle alone with my decision until summer, and never crossed her line of privacy. Talking to classmates would have confused me. She and I were first from our class to choose a religious vocation.

Lindy arrived at the convent a day before me. The sisters had a guesthouse where we spent our last night before officially entering the next morning. Sister Philomene showed us to our rooms in the two-story, white clapboard house. There were no other guests. The hardwood floors of the quiet, empty house creaked with every step we took. We could find no radio. Music would have muffled echoes in the hollow rooms. The bedroom furniture was comfortable but barely one-step removed from Academy dorm styles.

On our last night of freedom, no restrictions were imposed— not even a curfew. I expected some of our teachers to welcome us and share some last minute advice. We hadn't anticipated having the evening to ourselves.

One last fling at a bar was a thought, but neither of us drank, nor had we ever crossed the threshold of any Nauvoo tavern. We didn't smoke so there were no lingering cigarettes to finish. Our wildness extended to a hamburger and a chocolate food at Kraus's restaurant. Nauvoo had little to offer in the way of night life. We may have gone to a movie—I don't remember. The threat of Sister Rose catching me doing something wrong, causing me to be rejected at the last minute tempered any racy idea I might have had.

The official postulant uniform—black skirt, baggy black long-sleeved blouse, elbow length black cape, white plastic collar tied with a black shoestring—hung in the closet. We tried the outfit on for size, though size hardly mattered. The one-size-fits-all, Amish-looking costume camouflaged every hint of a figure. One size fit both of us, but at varying lengths. The cape looked short on Lindy's long arms, while my skirt fell well below my knees.

We had a sleepless night and morning came too soon. Sister Philomene knocked at the door to take us to morning prayers. She checked our capes, straightened our waist-length sheer black veils held in place with bobby pins and instructed us to cross our hands over our chests under the black cape. Only our faces were exposed. Sister Philomene nodded and smiled with approval. Like scared orphans, we followed her into the chapel where the entire community of sisters assembled for Lauds, the morning prayer of the Divine Office recited in Latin. The sisters chanted verses alternating from side to side in the chapel, sometimes standing and intermittently bowing toward the altar. Feeling nervous and conspicuous, we were ushered to the front pew and seated next to a few sisters wearing white veils. At their cue, Lindy and I jumped up and down, bowed, and tried to keep up with the meaningless verses. We had no understanding of the Latin verses. I wondered if anyone did. Perhaps Sister Dolores, who taught Latin, could understand it. The white-veiled sisters were novices. A year ago, they were new postulants, so they understood our awkwardness. Lindy and I were the newest members beginning the first step of a five-year formation process.

A novice beside me calmed my long-standing aversion to the front row in church. I feared not knowing what to do or when to move. That bit of anxiety was left over from pre-school days when my older brothers took me to church. I had marched up to the front row while my brothers sat in the back. Halfway through Mass one Sunday, while standing, as I thought I should, I heard a rustle of movement behind me and everyone *else* stood. I realized I had been the only one in the whole church standing—right in the front row. I was so little I could hardly be seen, but I was embarrassed at my mistake. Front row insecurity followed me forever.

With the help of the novices, Lindy and I muddled through morning prayers, then Mass, followed by half an hour of meditation. A novice handed each of us a book. All the sisters sat quietly with a book in hand—just reading, I figured. I wasn't in the mood to crack a new book, especially one not of my choosing. After little sleep, rising at 5:00 A.M. and spending two hours in chapel, I couldn't concentrate on reading anything. I was ready for breakfast, eager to see my teachers, and meet the other sisters.

A bell dinged from the back of chapel. Everyone rose and filed out, older sisters first, down the stairs to the refectory in the basement. The sisters lined up like dominoes around long, brown tables arranged in a U shape. Ushered to a table separate from the older sisters—like the *kids'* table on holidays at home—I spied my initialed silver napkin ring in the center of the table, nestled among several others. No sign of my mother's napkins, only a plain white cotton one rolled into the silver ring. The walls of the room were concrete block painted antiseptic white. Sunshine streaming through the high, narrow windows gave little warmth to the sterile room. All heads were bowed; hands hidden under the black garments. Lindy nudged me. I put my hands under my cape and stared at the linoleum floor. Mother Ricarda, the Superior, led grace before the meal. Chairs scraped across the floor and everyone sat. Feeling conspicuous and awkward in the silence, I searched the room for the familiar faces of my teachers. No one looked up. Following suit, I looked down quickly, wondering when we could talk or *if* we could talk. After what seemed an interminable silence, Mother Ricarda chanted, "Praised be Jesus and Mary."

"Now, and forever, Amen," The response erupted in unison followed by a burst of conversation and soft laughter. Finally, everyone was talking.

Lindy and I sat at a table with the novices who would be our closest companions for the next year. Novices and postulants make up the Novitiate, the first two years of formation in a nun's life. There were welcoming introductions and small talk around the table over a simple breakfast. Place settings of heavy white dishes and a mixture of flatware were at each place. Pitchers of orange juice, followed by plates of toast, butter pats on small white plates, and bowls of cereal made the rounds. A novice in a long white apron came around behind us with coffee. She carried two pots, one with black coffee and one with coffee already creamed. Cups were upside down. I learned to turn it over in time to get my coffee each morning as the server passed. The novices were cheerful and genuinely happy to welcome us.

When Mother Ricarda rang the little silver bell again, it signaled the end of the meal. Conversations stopped in mid-sentence and everyone stood for prayers. After prayer, the sisters gathered around the new *kids*, greeting and welcoming us with warm gestures of acceptance. I couldn't wait to talk with Sister Joann to share my feelings and first impressions. She was warm and loving, but a bit vague about when we might talk at length. The first surprise of many to follow was later explained by Sister Philomene.

The *Praised be Jesus and Mary* at breakfast announced a day of celebrating as new postulants were eased into the daily routine and silent world ahead. The mysterious ways, I once thought would be adventurous, were just beginning. So far, it wasn't the adventure I had expected, but it was still too early to judge.

I had no idea that every day in the convent was silent. As students, we never noticed that our teachers were never chatting with one another, except for a brief time after lunch or evening meals. They, of course, were always talking to us before, during, and after school. The dorm prefects spent hours talking and laughing with us. I learned that the only exceptions to the silence were special feast days, Christmas, and other holy days. The month of March had several "talking" feast days, feasts of St. Benedict—the founder of the Benedictines—St. Patrick and St. Joseph. Each day's celebration began at breakfast with the sweet words, *Praised be Jesus and Mary* that signaled permission to talk all day. With few exceptions—dinner on a sister's feast day and two brief periods in every day—all other times were silent. I wondered how I would be able to do that.

Postulants are addressed as "Miss," so I was now called *Miss* Mary Ann. The "Miss" title for postulants was meant to distinguish us from the girls we were before. I thought *it is going to take more than a Miss in front of my name to transform me from the girl I used to be.*

A gradual stripping of our individual identity had begun. We were being formed into model religious women. Uniformity became the norm, personal possessions taken away from us, family names dropped. Detachment from everything personal was being ingrained. The message was: *the more detached from things we were, the closer to God we would become.* I figured big portions of help from God would be necessary for me to manage the detachment thing.

Within days, Lindy and I were greeting new postulants. Helen, an Academy classmate joined us. Marmae and B.J., friends from another girls' school in Peoria, Ellen, an Academy graduate from Chicago entered after a year of college, and Pat, taught by the Benedictines in an Illinois grade school, enlarged our group. We were seven little Misses studying the origin of Benedictine monasteries and learning to be nuns.

I thought I had learned everything about a nun's life from living with the sisters night and day through four years of high school. I was wrong. Observing them in the classroom, seeing their happiness at recreational times, and admiring them at prayer revealed only a fraction of the story. I realized I knew little of their history and nothing of their rules.

St. Mary's Convent and Academy had a long history on the Mississippi River before I reached its banks. Sister Philomene often told stories of the first years of the community.

In the nineteenth century, there was a growing population in the upper Mississippi River Valley. In response to the influx of families from Europe, priests and bishops searched for religious sisters to open schools to instruct the children of immigrants.

In 1874, Nauvoo parish priest, Father A. J. Reimbold, requested Benedictine sisters from St. Scholastica Convent in Chicago to serve the educational needs of the parish children. Five nuns took a train to Burlington, Iowa, traveled down river by steamer and crossed into Illinois, arriving in Nauvoo in mid-October. Father Reimbold had arranged for them to purchase a house from a local Icarian vintner whose property went into liquidation due to a failed grape crop. The sisters opened what they first called St. Scholastica's Academy on a hill at the horseshoe bend of the river. It began as a day school, a mission branching from the Sisters of St. Benedict at St. Scholastica Convent in Chicago.

What would eventually become St. Mary's Academy opened with seven students. Besides religion, fundamentals of German, French, algebra, geometry, history, literature, painting, music, and household arts completed the curriculum. Within five years, enrollment at the new school increased, as did the number of sisters. In 1879, the growing community separated from St. Scholastica's community, and formed a new Motherhouse under the name of St. Mary's Convent and

Academy, independent of the Chicago community. The new convent fell under the approbation of Bishop John L. Spalding, first bishop of the diocese of Peoria, Illinois.

Though an independent congregation, the bishop of the diocese had authority over the sisters as to mission schools they would administer and even elections of their superiors. The Nauvoo parish priest was the bishop's local representative.

I knew a little of St. Benedict's life from classes at the Academy, but nothing of his Rule. As students, we learned of his life when the sisters celebrated his feast day in March, but the details of Benedict's Rule were not something we needed to know or cared about.

Sisters of the Order of St. Benedict—or Benedictines, as they are commonly called—date back to the sixth century. Benedict, a young Roman university student, retreated from the debauchery of Roman society to a cave on the cliffs outside the village of Subiaco to devote his life to seeking God. When others requested he teach them his way of life and how to follow his prayerful lifestyle, he established the Montecassino Monastery, south of Rome. Benedict's twin sister, Scholastica, admired her brother so much that she formed a community of women. They also followed his guidelines, which became known as the *Rule of Benedict*. Benedict's Rule is still used today in monasteries across the globe as a guide for respectful human interaction inspired by the Gospel.

It took me some time to appreciate Benedict's wisdom. I discovered his Rule was a manual on leading a monastic life of charity, prayer, and good works. In order to lead a peaceful life of prayer and meditation in his monastery of men, Benedict scheduled every hour of the day, times for meals, for silence, for work, and for prayer, leaving them no time for discord or competition. In Benedict's day, the regimentation and silence were his way of keeping peace among a variety of uncultured men. He understood that silence leads to a direct connection to God. That philosophy still works today in men and women's communities.

The women of St. Mary's Monastery (convent), came to Nauvoo from Chicago, but their community originated in Bavaria. Independently managed, they differ from other Benedictine houses across the country only in their primary ministry: the needs of the people. From the sixth century to the twenty-first, Benedict's common-sense approach to a life lived for God, whether as a religious or secular, Catholic or non-Catholic, still works. For some who search for the "something missing" in their lives, the Rule of Benedict can be the answer. Spirituality is not exclusive to those behind convent or monastery walls.

As time went by, I grew accustomed to my new life and began to take the rules and regulations in stride and accepted them as part of what I signed on for. We spent our days working, studying the Benedictine Rule, praying, and gaining weight on bread and grape jelly—a mid-morning snack eaten in silence. My anorexic look disappeared. Though silence was the norm, it was dispensed with for one hour of recreational talking after lunch and again each evening after dinner just before evening prayers. At evening recreation, we worked on projects, played games, and chatted until the clanging of the bell for Compline, the evening prayer before the great night silence. At the sound of the bell, all talking stopped immediately—in mid-sentence, mid-darning, mid-laughter. Often, laughing couldn't be stopped. Shoulders still shook through Compline. Sudden silence made the joke funnier. Benedict would not have approved. *On hearing the signal for an hour of the divine office, the monk will immediately set aside what he has in hand and go with utmost speed, yet with gravity and without giving occasion for frivolity. (Rule, Ch. 43)*

A designated Sunday visit from my parents was the highlight of each month.

"You look good," my mother offered as we hugged, "you've put some weight on your bones." I certainly had done that. Even the one-size-fits-all skirt was snug.

Postulants had the privilege of leaving the grounds for an afternoon, but we were not allowed to go out to dinner. Not that I wanted to be seen in a public restaurant in my conspicuous outfit. Usually we visited on the convent grounds. It pleased my dad to take me out for a picnic to a city park across the river in Keokuk, Iowa. We went down to Lock and Dam No. 19 on the river where we watched a long barge move in. Water filled the cavity lifting the barge to the top of the dam. As though taking a giant step up, the barge exited out the other side. The navigational marvel fascinated us.

Mother got out her trusty little Brownie box camera and took several pictures of me to show family and friends my new outfit. The time was too short. We had to be back at the convent in time for evening prayers before supper. My parents missed me, but they were relieved to see I looked healthy and happy. I always looked forward to the few hours of family time each month. I couldn't get enough news of my brothers, friends, and every morsel of what was happening in Bement. In a way, it made me sad to know life was going on without me. I missed everyone and everything, and looked forward to an occasional freedom from the convent enclosure, but my life was going on also. Joy and peace filled every day. I grew close to my classmates as we lived and worked together without dissension. I was adapting to the rigorous schedule, the silence, and frequent prayer. I felt contented with my life.

Chapter Nine – *The Novitiate*

$$\equiv$$

N ovitiate days were filled with *Ora et Labora,* the motto of St. Benedict's Rule—*Prayer and Work.* Benedict recognized that work, as well as prayer, can be a way to God. There are times for organized prayer and times for scheduled work—both were valued as part of the spiritual path. *Idleness is the enemy of the soul. Therefore, the brothers should have specified periods for manual labor as well as for prayerful reading.* (Rule, Ch. 48)

Everyone was expected to work in some capacity. We learned the value of work, not only as a contribution to the welfare of all, but also as a time to develop a personal relationship with God. Communication with God was not relegated to chapel time. Work was considered as sacred as prayer. It was not just a job.

No one looked down on the sister who mopped floors or cleaned toilets because everyone, young and old, drew those duties at some time. Older members who could no longer teach or do manual labor, were given tasks of preparing mailings, or cutting S & H stamps to be collected and redeemed for silverware. We were a family, each carrying a portion of the load.

Sister Martha, the coupon queen, had a team of sisters who regularly gathered at a table in the big community room every day.

Their *labora* consisted of cutting, counting, and organizing the General Mills box-top coupons. At another table, Sister Fabian's helpers prepared mailings for the Dollar-A-Year Club. One dollar at a time, Sister Fabian, the treasurer, helped restore the community to solvency after earlier days of bankruptcy. Sister Innocents humbled herself by begging donations and selling raffle tickets for handmade items contributed by the sisters. As one of the older sisters, she had experienced the severe community hardships of an earlier time.

I often drove Sister Innocents on her begging missions, humbling myself right along with her. As an Academy girl, I volunteered to drive, but as a postulant, I was volunteered. We walked up one side of Main Street and down the other into store after store in the towns along the Mississippi. The fact that no one knew me in the towns on the Iowa side of the river where we begged saved me from total embarrassment. Sister Innocents was well named; she had the sweetest, angelic face. Storeowners found her innocent smile and soft, pleading voice difficult to turn down. She stood her ground and came out victorious even when it was obvious the victim had no intention of donating. As a student, I could fade into the surroundings, pretending not to know her, but as a postulant, I was easily pegged as her partner in the shakedown.

In the early 1900s, the community had become the victim of an unscrupulous financial adviser who advocated a huge building expansion. The country's financial crash in late 1907 left the community penniless. The sisters vowed never again to be so near insolvency and at risk of the frightening possibility of disbanding. As postulants, we sometimes heard vague references to the hardships suffered by those who cut coupons or begged, but they never admonished us with stories of "in my day . . .' When I later learned the true story of the near financial disaster they suffered, my youthful embarrassment at begging seemed minor. Without their courage through deprivation, there may not have been a St. Mary's Academy for me to attend.

Nevertheless, scrubbing floors and cleaning toilets was not what I had in mind when I sought the life of service. Some thought we were little more than worker bees that kept the convent running. I understood that, as the young ones in the family, we would do the least favorite jobs and had no expectation that outside help would be hired for housework, garden work, laundry, or cooking. That was not Benedict's teaching.

Sister Emmanuel, a native of Ireland, approached her duty of dust mopping halls to a level of religious fanaticism. She would swish her mop at us postulants with a frown on her furrowed face and a twinkle in her eye if we obstructed her path. She seldom spoke; she may have only known Gaelic. As the unsubstantiated story goes, she came from Ireland with her cousins, who had been visiting relatives in their homeland, and when it came time for her to return to her Irish community, they didn't want her back. She may have been a bit quirky in her seriousness, but she was deeply religious. When not mopping floors, she could be found filling holy water fonts or on her knees in the chapel with arms outstretched in prayer.

Once a month prior to afternoon Vespers, the sisters lined up in the hallway outside the chapel for a devotion to the Little Infant Jesus of Prague. Sister Emmanuel always prepared the small statue of the Little Infant for a procession. She removed the two-foot statue from its pedestal, dressed it with a ruby red velvet cape trimmed in ermine, and placed it on a cloth-covered platform braced by two long padded boards for hoisting onto shoulders. Four postulants or novices were delegated to carry the statue in procession through the halls of the convent, up and down stairs, with all of the sisters following and singing a song in adoration of Jesus. Balancing the statue and keeping it level while climbing stairs was tricky, especially for new novices, as yet unaccustomed to navigating stairs in their long skirts. Sister Emmanuel never joined the procession. Her mission was to clear the way for the entourage. Wearing her soft, flat, leprechaun-like shoes, she sprinted ahead of the lead carriers, opening doors and shaking a finger to shush away anyone lingering in the path. Her old bones would spring up the stairs ahead of the procession—sometimes crawling under the statue and between the carriers to rush toward a closed door at the top of the stairs. In her fervor for the Little Infant of Jesus, she allowed no disruption to the progress of the parade. Postulants carrying the statue and those following would begin to shake with laughter at her pious antics. The poor Little Infant Jesus tottered precariously. He must have been laughing with us—or at us—while hanging on for dear life. The procession ended back at the chapel. The superior led prayers asking the Infant Jesus "to bless us and send us pupils and postulants."

Benedict was a lay person, not a priest; laymen followed him. They prayed together and worked together. *When they live by the labor of their hands, as our ancestors and the apostles did, then they are really monastics.* (Rule, Chap. 48)

We definitely lived "by the labor of our hands." Summers brought mornings of strawberry picking. Novices, postulants, and any sister available, headed to the strawberry patch after breakfast—early enough to beat the heat. With little black capes and white collars removed, we grabbed our colorful mini-print work aprons and walked to the strawberry patch down the hilly street to the flats along the river—the original Mormon settlement. The owner of the patch donated his end-of-season surplus berries to the convent for the picking. We picked strawberries by the tons. Outdoor work gave me a closer-to-God feeling; better than cleaning toilets. Toilets, however, increased my humility.

"There will be an all-day strawberry bee tomorrow in the basement. Go directly to the basement after breakfast," Sister Philomene announced at evening recreation.

A bee, what's a bee? We soon learned. At harvest time, there were a series of "bees"—a corn "bee," grape "bee," strawberry "bee," and many other kinds of "bees" to prepare fruits and vegetables for canning and making jellies. Old and young gathered in the basement. Seated on straight chairs arranged in circles, wearing our long print aprons, we rolled up our sleeves and went to work: culling strawberry stems, breaking green beans, shelling peas, and stripping husks of corn by the bushels for canning. Only the Hail Marys of the rosary, said in unison, broke the silence.

At my first bee, sitting in a circle with other postulants, shucking endless ears of sweet corn in silence the scene struck me as funny. It didn't take much in the unnatural silence to set us off in giggles. One screech from Marmae, our delicate city girl, at the sight of a worm in the silk of an ear of corn, and we were gone. Marmae flipped the infested ear; Lindy grabbed it, broke off the wormed end, and tossed it. The rosary resumed, the quiet giggles continued. Marmae's production slowed as she peeked gingerly into each ear of corn. Lofty, contemplative thoughts were shattered for any of us who might have had them.

Every Tuesday morning after prayers and before breakfast, postulants and novices walked the long block between convent and academy, past the grape vineyard to the institutional laundry in the basement of St. Joe Hall dormitory. Beyond the vineyard on our hill, we could see the river embracing the peninsula of Nauvoo along the flats. I never tired of the changing nature of the river as it followed the seasons. It was a symbol of both tranquility and endurance, a natural meditation prompt.

Postulants and novices made up the laundry crew assigned to do the wash for the sisters and academy students. In spite of the long day in a steamy workplace, the break in the routine of the week was a welcome diversion. Sister Fabian, community treasurer and council member, managed the laundry workday, assigning us to jobs as needed. She worked right alongside us while she led the rosary; we responded in unison with the second half of the prayer. The rosary broke the monotony of the droning institutional-size machines. Sister Fabian was careful to rotate the jobs so that we could sit at the folding tables now and then. We took turns having breakfast and lunch in the back room. At noon, Sister Fabian announced an hour of recreation with our favorite phrase, "Praised be Jesus and Mary." Chatter began, but the work did not stop.

Two of us stood at the mangle, feeding wet sheets into the big pressing machine, one at each end of the twelve-foot, canvas-covered rollers. Two others caught the hot pressed sheets tumbling from below the mangle, ready for folding. The folders called out "over" or "under" when spying the sorting label indicating which side should be up. By the time one sheet was folded and stacked, another dropped, ready to fold.

Every corner of the room had washing, drying, pressing machines, and long tables for folding. The sounds of sudsy water whirling in huge washers, steam escaping from presses, wheels of wooden bins filled with wet or dry clothes rolling over concrete filled the steamy air. We kept the tasks flowing in rhythm, like little Keebler cookie elves happily working in unison. Feeding the mangle was a monotonous job. After rising so early and working in the heat of the room, it was easy to become drowsy.

Miss Ellen and Sister Monica took their turn working the large mangle, feeding sheets into it one by one. The heat and the rhythm of the process while we said the rosary could be mesmerizing, especially after lunch. Alert, Sister Monica saw a sheet that needed straightening. Her small hand reached for it and moved too far into the steaming mangle. The mangle caught her hand pulling it with the wet sheet over the canvas roller into the hot press. A painful groan from Sister Monica broke the silence. Frantic, Miss Ellen thrust her hand to the metal safety guard stopping the forward movement. It was too late.

We all knew how to stop the rolling of the press, but no one, not even Sister Fabian, knew how to release the pressure of the rollers allowing Sister Monica to remove her hand. Henry, our faithful plant manager, was called. Sister Fabian stood by Sister Monica, supporting her limp frame until Henry arrived and released her.

Everyone paled and froze in shock. In a panic to do something, I ran out of the laundry and up to the academy to get Sister Bernarda, the convent and school nurse. She was already on her way down to administer whatever relief she could to ease Sister Monica's pain. My throat tightened with fear—I couldn't talk. The trauma all but paralyzed our crew. Sister Fabian sent us all to the back room to wait. The rest of the day we prayed the rosary for Sister Monica and to calm our own fears.

To this day, Miss Ellen says, "I still remember that awful groan; never heard anything like it before or since. It was pure pain."

Sister Philomene regularly visited Sister Monica in the Iowa City hospital. One day she asked me to drive her. I didn't really want to go, afraid of seeing Monica and not knowing what to expect or what to say. Awake and smiling, she greeted us when we walked in. Her right arm stretched out from the bed with her hand resting in a rectangular shaped incubator-like container next to the bed. Open from the top, a lamp inside exposed her hand.

"I was very lucky," she said. "It was only my hand."

I looked at her, at the room, and everywhere but at the box, for fear of seeing her hand or what was left of it.

"Don't look at it if you don't want, you might feel faint," she said.

If she could be that brave, I felt I could look. I might share her suffering for one moment. My knees weakened as I looked at her shriveled fingers, flat and brown. Her hand could not be saved. I thought she had to be lonely and scared in that hospital so far away from her Peoria home. I would have been begging for my mother. Sister Monica was the bravest young person I had ever seen. I'll never forget her courage.

There were five prayer times a day in chapel for the recitation of Psalms, known as the Liturgy of the Hours. Early morning Lauds lasted the longest. At midday we came together for Terce and Sext, before lunch, and None after lunch. Evening Vespers were before dinner and Compline before the great night silence. In between prayer times, we worked at any and all tasks necessary to maintain the large institution. In addition to the laundry, duties included weeding the gardens, serving meals, washing dishes, washing and waxing floors, and polishing the four-story convent building from top to bottom. We never went to the fifth floor; it was basically the attic, though Sister Edmond and Sister Modesta chose to live up there. It always reminded me of something out of *Jane Eyre*. My wild imagination pictured Sister Edmond as an ethereal Grace Poole.

Serving the meals could have its benefits. There was a small cooler in the sink room where we washed serving bowls after each meal. Separated from the kitchen, the sink room had room for only two or three servers at a time. The pint-sized refrigerator cooler was large enough for the two or three bottles of altar wine kept there for Mass. The sacristan sister prepared the cruets (small decanter-type bottles) for Mass each morning. As postulants, we joked about having a sample now and then. One morning after breakfast, the temptation became too great for Lindy, Marmae, and me. From our sink room vantage point, we could see that the coast was clear. While one of us kept watch, we took turns having a sip of wine. The thrill of the deed turned out to be far better than the taste of the wine. We kept what we thought was *our* secret, but somehow the novice in charge of preparing the altar wines realized the quantity in the bottle was lower than it should have been. By a process of elimination, she deduced the wine was missing after our shift.

By the time Sister Philomene learned of our transgression and called us into her office one by one—we had already forgotten it. I sat nervously on the short-legged, antique chair, which put me in an inferior position, sitting almost knee to knee with Sister. I had been in her tiny office many times before, usually on my knees asking for a penance for a transgression of the Rule, other times for scheduled counseling conferences. This command performance was unexpected. "Is there something that you would like to tell me, Miss Mary Ann?" she asked.

"I'm not sure, Sister. Is there something I have done?"

I was stumped as to what I needed to tell her until she enlightened me. I had to admit to drinking the altar wine, and ask for a penance. Individually and in private, we each knelt before her, asked for a penance, and received a lecture—a small price to pay for the thrill of drinking the wine.

As postulants, we were spared the humiliation of kneeling before the entire community in the dining room to confess our faults and ask Mother Superior for a penance. Dining room humility was reserved for professed sisters. Such a public humiliation as a postulant would probably have been enough to consider picking up my napkin ring and leaving. I remember my shock the first time I saw one of the sisters kneel down in the center of the dining room, in front of the head table, holding a dish and asking a penance for breaking it. I couldn't believe it. She obviously had not broken it on purpose. Breaking a dish was considered careless destruction of community property and called for a penance to make amends. *Whoever fails to keep the things belonging to the monastery clean or treats them carelessly should be reproved.* (Rule, Ch. 32)

Sister Antonia was an intellectual with a sense of humor and a reputation for being distinctly individual in a house of commonality. One time at the beginning of the evening meal, she made her entrance into the dining room, walked up to the head table, in front of Mother Ricarda. An uncharacteristic muffling of commotion stirred among the sisters. I looked up and saw Sister Antonia carrying a broken toilet seat. Stifled coughing erupted all around the dining room. With a penitent face, she knelt before everyone and asked for a penance. Knowing Sister Antonia, I suspect she did it on a dare. I didn't know how Mother Ricarda kept a straight face or was able to admonish her.

Weeks went by and I still had not visited with Sister Joann, my mentor in high school. A major revelation came when I learned of the regulation forbidding postulants and novices to talk with the rest of the community at any time. I thought it an incredulous and stupid rule. I was not allowed to talk to Sister Joann, the person who encouraged me to follow in her footsteps. An occasional nod and a smile at mealtime were the only acknowledgements between us. Happy times, sad times, or my impressions of convent life, were not to be shared with my friend. Silence was one thing, but never visiting with the teacher who had become a dear friend during those four years of high school struck me as ridiculous. I was crushed. I wanted to ask her why she hadn't shared that policy with me before I entered. My vocation probably wouldn't have been deterred by it, but at least I would have been warned.

If there was some value to that regulation, it was lost on me. We were not given a reason at the time, but later I learned the policy was meant to protect the young people from getting conflicting messages or being bombarded by corrections from older sisters. It was a carryover from historic times in the convents of Europe, as were many of the regulations and customs adopted through the centuries. The custom deprived us of the experience and wisdom of older sisters. I would love to have known some of them better. I wanted to know their stories—where they came from, why they entered, and what it was like in their early convent days.

The aroma of meals reached the dining room before the three-shelved metal cart rolled in, pushed by two postulants or novices. Serving dishes for every six sisters were passed family style. At first, serving meals in silence was a challenge. We presented the dishes in perfect synchronization, to the head of each table, beginning with Mother Ricarda. After the first passing, the dishes were picked up, taken to the kitchen for refills, and passed again for seconds. We took our timing cue from Mother Ricarda. A nod from her indicated desserts should be passed. The empty serving dishes were picked up and returned to the kitchen.

At another nod, we hauled in a cart stacked with blue and gray porcelain pans and spatulas for scraping individual plates. Once the food was scraped into the pans—which seemed like a gross practice at the table—pans filled with hot soapy water were passed. All dishes were washed in concert, dried, and set back in place, ready for the next meal. Napkins were folded in the personal napkin rings and placed in the center of the table. I thought the dish scraping and washing of plates at the table was weird. The simplest mishap—a splash of soapy water in a lap—could send me and Marmae, my dishwashing partner, into giggles. Fits of laughter that erupt while everyone is sitting in sober silence, are nearly impossible to stop.

When Mother Ricarda tapped the bell, everyone stood for after-meal prayers. The long row of sisters ascended the stairs like a human ribbon of black and white unfolding toward the chapel for another chanting of the divine office.

Waitressing had never been one of my aspirations. I never had, nor wanted a summer job as a waitress. In my first days of serving in the silent basement dining room I encountered a minor challenge or two. I couldn't always interpret the sign language. Juggling vintage blue enamelware coffee pots filled with hot java—one with cream, one without—in each hand was challenging. I soon learned coffee preferences of each sister. I was feeling pretty confident in keeping the preferences straight when Sister Immanuel, our Irish eccentric, shook her head at me with a frown on her face, lips pursed. She wanted neither of the coffees I carried, but her cup was upright indicating she wanted something in it.

Annoyed that I could not interpret her signals, she whispered, "Hot water!"

I wondered if I heard the Irish brogue right. My quizzical look caused her to break silence and repeat, "Hot water!"

"Could she really want plain hot water?" I asked novice Sister Denise in the kitchen.

"Yes, there's a pot of hot water on the cart, pour that in her cup." I thought this must be one of those blind obediences meant to test me. Following the directive, I got a smile from Sister Emmanuel, and discovered there were others who preferred hot water. "Good for the digestion," I was told.

That fit right in with another custom and health benefit. Sister Philomene neglected to warn us of the practice until we were faced with the small dish of shimmering golden pills passed at breakfast one winter morning. Trustingly, we followed the novices lead, took a pill and swallowed it blindly. I almost gagged when told the small translucent pills contained cod liver oil. A pill a day at breakfast was meant to keep us healthy through cold winters.

Convents across the country followed similar rules and rituals. There were, and still are, varying degrees of rigidity in their practices. Benedictine communities were typically small in number and based on a family structure. As young postulants and novices in the novitiate, we were the children, treasured by all. Though she tried, Sister Philomene was not naturally loving or motherly. Her attempts to show a warm side of her personality were awkward and it came off as insincere. I knew she cared, but often I longed for my mother's affection.

Larger communities often had novitiates numbering more than our entire Benedictine house. Their novices and postulants were housed in separate buildings from the rest of their community. Convents with their own colleges provided their sisters a college education during the first years of formation, thus completing their degrees and readying them for teaching, nursing, or the work of their community. While teacher training before entering a classroom was a huge benefit, separation from the rest of the community had its drawbacks. Young Sisters had little opportunity to get to know others in their community.

Our Nauvoo community was small enough that we knew all the sisters who lived at the convent, even if we didn't converse with them. We served them, not only in the dining room, but in the infirmary in their sickbeds. We were taught to respect them as family elders.

No matter the size or the work of the communities from one order to another, the patterns of daily living were similar. The secrecy of life inside the convent walls was universal, not to be shared outside. Not that I would want to tell my parents about scraping dishes and washing them at the table, or about the penances received on our knees for breaking a dish, or that we could not talk to our teachers anymore, or the practice of silence, or that in the name of poverty and detachment we could not keep a gift. Even a box of candy was turned in to be kept in the larder and shared with others during recreation. The novitiate larder, another tempting place, was the cupboard next to the novitiate recreation room where food treats were kept, but never touched, unless Sister Philomene offered them to us at recreation.

Some secrets were better kept within the convent walls. Who would understand such rules? My mother would never have believed that I voluntarily put a cod liver oil pill in my mouth each morning. I never wanted her to know that I couldn't use the silverware she bought for me. Aside from the secrecy and antiquated practices, religious communities consist of ordinary people with ordinary quirks and idiosyncrasies. Personalities do not disappear with a vow ceremony. Uniformity did not turn us into a form of religious Stepford wives.

The convent kitchen, between the convent and academy dining rooms, served as a filter for academy faculty when transitioning from a dining room of chattering teenage girls to a silent dining room of sisters. Sister Walburga and her kitchen crew turned out meals for both dining rooms—sisters and girls. When I helped in the kitchen, Sister Walburga kept her crossed eyes on each person's task, giving directions. It wasn't easy for me to determine if she was addressing me or another sister. More than once, I embarrassed her and myself.

At work in the meal preparation room, I could catch a glimpse, a nod, and a smile from my favorite teachers, Sister Joann, Sister Veronica, and Sister Immaculata as they passed through. I disappeared when the heavy footsteps and large presence of Sister Rose filled the swinging double doors into the kitchen. Maybe it was my imagination, but I detected that the professed sisters in the kitchen felt the earth quake a bit too. Sister Rose's domineering effect reached me even when I was beyond her jurisdiction.

Classrooms for our studies were on the second floor of the convent. The silence in the building magnified the recognizable footsteps of Sister Rose as they drew closer to the classroom. In a class of postulants, I felt removed from the threat of being in trouble with her, but my stomach still tightened at the sound of her footsteps. The familiarity brought back the queasy feeling that overcame me when Sister Rose approached my freshmen religion class at the Academy. It took me back to high school and the day I was accused of cheating on a test.

"Mary Ann Cahill, keep your eyes on your own paper." I don't know why my desk didn't collapse through the floor; I wanted it to. I shriveled with humiliation, never daring to challenge her. Sister Rose had the power to make me feel guilty, even when I wasn't. As a postulant, I felt safe from her grasp, but not from her reach. When in her presence, she still could reach into my fragile psyche. Her imperious methods could whittle my confidence down to the size of a toothpick. I sat in the convent classroom, devoid of stimulation, dreading Education 101 with her as my professor.

The mission of Nauvoo Benedictines is teaching. Our introduction to becoming teachers was the course, Principles of Education, Education 101, which put me squarely under Sister Rose's discerning eye once again. She strode into the room, carrying under her arm the largest textbook I had ever seen. The volume was huge, the subject dry, and the professor had an unmatched zeal for imparting her love for education. Our lack of jubilation for the class never dampened her spirit. With her hands tucked in her belt, she would pace the floor, expounding on the glories of education, oblivious to her less-than-mesmerized students. Born to be an educator, she was also a powerful figure. I knew the sisters had a healthy respect for her authority, but I hadn't yet felt the full power of her position in the community. I thought I was safe from her.

Chapter Ten – *The Black Chips*

===

*A*t the end of each day, with my duties completed, supper served, and dishes washed, I looked forward to gathering in the novitiate room for an hour of recreation—talking. When sunshine spilled through the tall windows, the large room with hardwood floors brightened. Furnishings were stark—three long, wooden tables with straight-back chairs placed in U formation. There were no soft chairs, radios, TV, books, magazines, or newspapers to enjoy. Sister Philomene sat at the head of the table and joined in chatter with us— seven postulants and eight novices. We laughed a lot about things that had happened during the day when we couldn't talk. Barren as the surroundings were, we accepted the sterile atmosphere, though I would have enjoyed collapsing into a comfortable, overstuffed chair after a long day of classes and physical labor.

On Wednesday evenings, novices took their laundered coifs, the starched and pleated white linen garments worn around the face, and prepared them for wearing each day of the week. A length of white thread sewn through the pleats gave stability to the starched fabric. The threading of the pleats was very important in hot weather. When the humidity was high, the linen fabric coifs could droop if not reinforced by threading. An unpleated, sagging coif resembled multiple chins.

Another domestic art foreign to me was repairing holes in the toes of our black stockings. A hole was no reason to discard them. A wooden darning egg pushed into the toe of the stocking held it taut. The sisters taught us to use a large-eyed needle and black darning thread to crisscross a perfect basket weave, forming a closed grid over the hole. Perfection took patience. A hasty job left a lump of thread at the toe that could cripple a person. The neat weave of coal black, darning thread remained visible after multiple washings— contrasting with the black stockings that faded to green. We rolled the opaque stockings down to just below the knee, twisted the roll to one side and secured it in a knot under our mid-calf, black skirts. It worked, at least for most of us.

Sister Andrew, a novice older than most of us, never mastered the knack of keeping any of the garb on straight. Nor could she successfully roll her stockings. With the pleats of her coif often sagging to her chest on a hot summer day, she was a blustery blur moving down the narrow halls and across the large, institutional rooms with her black stockings a bundle around her ankles, her shoestrings often untied. Sister Andrew was a dedicated woman, impatient to attack the business of becoming a nun. Living with immature postulants must have annoyed her. As hard as she tried to follow the regimented life, no one was particularly surprised when she decided the solemn, silent, and slow lifestyle was not for her.

Like most young people who enter into a religious community, I expected to stay. I didn't see religious life as something I would just try out for a while to see if I liked it. For me it was a forever commitment from the day I said goodbye to my parents at the convent door.

I soon learned that admittance into the religious community as a postulant was but the first stage of acceptance. When Mother Ricarda admitted me to the novitiate, it was not a confirmation that I had a religious vocation. For me, the fact that I struggled with my decision to enter, and then chose to do so, meant I did have a vocation.

I soon learned that the novitiate years are not only years of formation, but also of discernment. While some postulants and novices were contemplating a decision to stay or to go, we all were being evaluated by the community as to our suitability for religious life.

Keeping the rules in the novitiate was not difficult for me—for the most part. There were not a lot of rules in my family. My brothers and I knew what was expected and we didn't cross the line, thereby avoiding disappointment for our parents. With this background, following the convent rules was easy, even those I might have wanted to question, but challenging the rules was not an option.

I went blissfully along day-to-day, never feeling the threat of being sent home should I not measure up. If I wasn't talking during recreation time, I was singing. One afternoon as we weeded the novitiate garden on hands and knees, I sang to myself. The garden was a sunken area down the hill from the backyard of the convent nearest the novitiate wing. Novices and postulants had the duty to keep the flower beds weeded. A statue of Mary, the Blessed Mother of Jesus, stood at the end of the garden walk bordered with a rainbow of Portulacas that bloomed each morning and closed up in the evening. The peaceful garden made a perfect meditation spot. The song I sang was not exactly meditative.

"Miss Mary Ann, I don't believe singing that song is exemplary of nunly decorum," Sister Philomene volunteered as she worked among us.

"Sorry, Sister," I responded, shrinking in humiliation. I decided my singing was best confined to chapel or choral group.

It never occurred to me that singing to the happy beat of Hank Williams's "Jambalaya" was off base. I could tell from the tone of her voice it was an indiscretion that called for a penance later. A penance request from a superior in a convent was not the same as a penance requested from a priest, God's representative, in a confessional. The confessional was reserved for transgressions against the Ten

Commandments or of the Seven Sins of pride, avarice, lust, anger, gluttony, envy, or sloth. In the convent, penances were requested for disregard of community rules—breaking the great night silence, habitual talking during silence, disregard of community property, or showing a lack of religious decorum by singing a Hank Williams song of romance.

Procrastinating as long as I could without irritating Sister Philomene, I swallowed my pride, and knocked on her office door.

"Come," she responded.

"May I speak with you, Sister?"

"Yes, Sister, come sit."

Instead of sitting, I got down on my knees in front of her and humbly asked for a penance for something that I didn't think was that big a deal.

"Sister, may I have a penance for singing an inappropriate song in the garden?"

The penance was often just a lecture on what St. Benedict, our founder, would expect as proper behavior, or sometimes she would assign some act to make amends for the indiscretion, like giving the toilets an extra scrub or an extra hour of pulling the garden weeds in silence. The humiliation was meant to make us holier and closer to suffering as Jesus did. I kept telling myself that, but I don't believe it made me any holier—the transgressions were not sins. No matter what I thought, "Jambalaya" called for a penance of saying an entire rosary on my knees in the chapel.

Sister Philomene was new to her position as Novice Mistress; we were her first group of postulants. I doubt any one of the sisters sought the position. All her recreational moments had to be spent with us. Taking teenagers out of the world and attempting to make holy, obedient, religious sisters of them must have been a challenge. To make her job even more difficult, she followed in the footsteps of Sister Mary Paul, beloved by her postulants and novices. I think

Sister Philomene was as uncomfortable as we were with the penance practice. It is one thing to receive a penance, but to sit in judgment of someone else for breaking a dish had to be humbling as well. She never kept us on our knees long. We learned how to fulfill our roles as religious sisters from her, not so much from her inspiration as from her sincerity, her example, and her strict adherence to the rules.

Though I deserved a few penances now and then, I never feared being sent home because of my indiscretions, nor did I ever consider going home. What an embarrassment that would have been to my parents and what a failure I would have been in my own eyes. I wasn't a perfect postulant yet, but I had grown more and more comfortable with my life.

When the first of our postulant group left to go back home, we were shocked. B.J. was with us only a few months when she decided religious life was not for her, and she returned home. She slipped away secretly without saying goodbye to any of us. We learned she had wanted to say goodbye, but rules forbade it. Secrecy was a common practice in most religious communities in those days. Saying goodbye and keeping in touch were discouraged, lest it upset those of us remaining. The secrecy surrounding the sudden and unexplained departure of our friends was abnormal; it probably did more damage to the resolve of our vocation than shedding a few goodbye tears with B.J. We never received an explanation as to why she or others left. It was left to our imaginations.

Sister Philomene gave regular progress reports on each of us to Mother Ricarda. I was beginning to understand that even if I felt I had a vocation and wanted to stay, the community could conclude otherwise and send me home. As novice mistress, Sister Philomene held the responsibility for our formation; her word weighed heavily with the other sisters. We spent most of our time under her direction, and the community based its final decision of our acceptance or rejection on her reports. Acceptance meant we could take the next step to become novices.

Our Reception Day was approaching. We would not only receive the habit—the garb that all sisters wore—but we would receive our new religious name. During the novice year, our second year, studies would be more spiritual—less secular. I eagerly anticipated the day when I would officially be a nun dressed in the long habit and veil. I still romanticized about the long, flowing, black dress. The mystery of how it felt to wear the garb and what I would look like in it would be resolved on Reception Day.

Postulants and novices lived separately from the rest of the community in our own small wing of the large convent building. Since we could not talk to any of the professed sisters, their conclusions about our fitness for religious life were based on their observations of us at work and prayer, in addition to Sister Philomene's reports.

Before going forward into the novice year, an interview with Mother Ricarda was required. One by one, we formally requested the privilege of receiving the habit of a novice.

I approached her office with much more trepidation than when knocking on Sister Philomene's door. My knees knocking, I rapped on the door.

"Please come in, dear." Her office was large, but welcoming. Mother Ricarda was a small woman with a kind face, almost angelic.

"Thank you, Mother." I felt calmed by her voice.

"You have something to ask me, Sister?" she spoke as I knelt before her.

"I humbly ask your approval for the privilege of receiving the holy habit of the order of St. Benedict as a sister of this Benedictine convent."

She approved with a smile, then helped me up from my knees, giving me a few words of encouragement for the pending acceptance by the entire community.

Sister Philomene presented her report on each of us at a chapter meeting held in the summer when all sisters were home from teaching missions. After the report, each member voted secretly with a white chip to accept us, or a black chip to reject us, for the next step in our formation.

The first vote taken would be on Lindy, the first of us to arrive. Many of the sisters knew her quite well because she came to the Academy as a seventh grader, and her sister was already in the community. We figured Lindy would pass easily.

Lindy never shared a lot about her family. Occasionally, she spoke of her brothers out in New Mexico and her aunt, who was her guardian. She had a stern, sober countenance, easily mistaken for anger or sullenness. Sometimes it was no mistake. Residue from a hurt in her childhood rumbled deep down. Though a woman of few words, there were strong feelings hidden beneath that dark, serious countenance.

A seven-day retreat preceded the ceremony of Reception. We were to receive the results of the chapter meeting before going into the strict seven-day silence. Just days before retreat, the harsh hammer of judgment fell. The results of the chapter meeting were stinging for Lindy and another postulant. Sister Philomene must have suffered heartache when she had to tell them they would not be going forward with the rest of us. The question always remained as to whether the community held them back because of Sister's report or community judgments formed from observation?

Sister Philomene gathered the remaining four of us to explain that Lindy and Pat would not be joining us as novices for a few more months. The community needed more time to evaluate their readiness for reception of the habit. It was an unexpected blow to all of us. The four of us rejoiced at our own acceptance, though it was a bittersweet moment. It was another deep cut in Lindy's life, another scar to carry. She was no doubt more sure and more ready than most of us. The community could not have understood what a kind heart and dedicated soul her stern countenance camouflaged.

With humility, Lindy accepted the decision to wait; her loyalty never wavered throughout her life.

Some years later on a mission, I received news from the monastery that Sister Augustine (Lindy) had been diagnosed with multiple sclerosis.

As we walked and talked at the monastery that next summer, she said, "The doctor told me if I wasn't so physically fit, I would already be using a walker."

"Good thing we played all those basketball and baseball games, right?" I said.

She grinned. "Yep, sure is."

Over the years, she suffered pain from the multiple sclerosis that most others did not realize. She hid it well with her always serious face.

On June 24, 1954, Reception Day, only four of the original seven of us would receive the habit. B.J., who had gone home earlier, returned to see Ellen, Helen, Marmae, and I receive the habit. Lindy and Pat had to endure the ceremony in their postulant outfits. I don't know what great change of character or piety would make them eligible in those few extra months of waiting. I admired their perseverance and wondered how there could not be bitterness in their hearts. God must have blessed them with a large dose of grace. As the black chips fell, their humility grew.

Chapter Eleven – *Reception Day*

*R*eception Day was the convent equivalent of a bridal day, a day full of joy and anticipation. Four of us would symbolically become brides of Christ, giving our lives to him in his service. After ten months of the rigor of postulant formation, including academic and religious studies, and hours of prayer and work, we reached the level of discipline and decorum necessary to be a novice. The "engagement" period was over—I was ready to be a bride.

The ceremony was to be held at the parish church across the street from the Academy campus. Like any bride, we were all dressed in long, white gowns with white veils. Unlike most brides, our dresses were identical modest Grecian style gowns with long, flowing, split sleeves. They looked identical to robes from the costume room at school. I could have sworn we wore them for a Lenten play. A white cord tied at the waist revealed a shape we hadn't shown in months. The sheer, white veil covered our heads and down to our waists. Sister Innocents prepared bouquets of flowers cut from her garden. Each of us invited a friend or family member to be our bridesmaids. They wore light blue formals. My cousin Margaret was my attendant.

Customary pictures were taken in the convent parlor before the ceremony. With faces scrubbed shiny, not a hint of makeup, our hair curled to look its best one last time, we were presented for the pictures. First a picture with my parents, proud, but nervous as to what kind of life I had chosen. The four of us posed with Sister Philomene and Mother Ricarda smiling happily at growth to their community. Flashbulbs sparked from all directions. The last picture was taken with our attendants, who looked beautiful in blue with rosy makeup that contrasted with our pale faces, starving for a hint of blush. The sun had little chance to tan us through the blackness we'd worn from head to toe for the last ten months.

The photo shoot was to pacify our families. Once we received the habit and white veil, no pictures would be allowed for the duration of our novice year. I never heard an explanation of that custom. The picture every family wanted most was of their daughter wearing her new habit. After reception day—marking the beginning of a year of seclusion—no one would see us to take our picture anyway, so I wondered why deprive the family of a keepsake picture?

My mother never went anywhere without her trusty Brownie box camera. Rule or no rule, she would not be stopped from sneaking snapshots now and then as I pretended not to notice. Of course, *posing* for a picture would have been too conspicuous—and vain.

My aunts and uncles, brothers, cousins, Linda and her mom gathered in the church with the other families. Most of the sisters were home from missions for the big occasion. They anticipated welcoming new novices into the community and learning our new names.

The church bells rang out announcing the procession. Organ music floated into the street, voices of the sisters sang in chorus. My heart was pounding as I began the walk of my life. Margaret, dressed in the requisite light blue formal, preceded me down the aisle. Searching for my parents, I caught a glimpse as I passed. Mother sat erect, with a smile on her face and winked at me. Dad had a sober expression; he couldn't quite muster a smile.

Halfway through the Mass at the Offertory, each of us received a large tray with a new black habit and white veil folded up on it. We marched with deliberation down the aisle, out of the church to the building where we changed from the white gown and veil to the black habit and white veil. The excitement and contrasting solemnity scrambled the butterflies in my stomach.

I was not yet nineteen. If I was to back out of this life commitment, this was the time to bolt. Even though I still knew little of what lay ahead of me, becoming a nun was the fulfillment of my heart's dream. After ten months of preparation for this day, I was not about to back out.

No doubt my parents had their own conflicting emotions of pride, joy, and sadness. As I walked out of the church, they caught one last glimpse of me, the last they would see of me before my transformation into a nun. My four brothers, relatives, and friends, had traveled far to witness this milestone in my life. Everyone waited in the church for our return. We were whisked off to the Villa Marie residence hall next to the church. The stripping down of the girl postulant into the novice nun began with the help of a sister who guided us in putting on the new garb. I had asked Sister Joann to help me. In addition to the long wool habit folded on the tray, there was the white coif to be wrapped around my head, concealing all but my face, and topped with a starched band of linen and a white veil. Keeping our hair tucked under the coif and band was tricky. Sister Joann cut some of the longer, pesky strands that kept creeping out. For a nun, having strands of hair sticking out around your face is like having your underwear show.

Wardrobe complete, we stepped out of the rooms, pointing and laughing, as we saw one another dressed for the first time as sisters.

Unlike normal brides, we had the opportunity to choose three names from any of the saints, but Mother Ricarda would make the final decision for us. There could be no duplicate names.

Like smitten teenagers, who practiced writing their boyfriends' names, we practiced writing the sister names we preferred.

"How do you like Sister Mary Joy, or Sister Madonna?" I asked. We spent evening recreations practicing the names. Madonna, Mary Joy, and Mary Magdalen were my final choices. Sister Joy might not have been accepted since it is not a saint's name.

"I'm pretty sure I want Mary Magdalen," I remember telling my parents.

I wanted them to get used to the idea, though the final choice would not be mine.

As always, my dad wanted to do all he could to grant my wishes. There was so little he could give me anymore, he tried to use leverage with his friend, Sister Martha, whom he had gotten to know when he gave her a ride from the monastery to her convent in Ivesdale.

"He asked me to do what I could to get you that name," Sister Martha told me. She'd given him a wink and a promise to do her best.

Little did he know that Sister Martha had no say in the decision, though I suspect she did convey the message to Mother Ricarda.

First in rank, I stood before the priest at the altar resigned to hear any name—knowing that Mother Ricarda had the authority to disregard my preferences and bestow a name of her choosing upon me. I still prayed for my first choice. Father Labonte pronounced the new names with a vigor that even the hearing impaired could understand.

"Miss Mary Ann Cahill, you will henceforth be known as Sister Mary Magdalen of the Mother of God." Breathing a sigh of relief and wearing a big smile, I returned to my seat, joyous and distracted.

Daddy took credit for one last gift to me, my new name.

Helen took the name, Sister Beatrice, Ellen became Sister Rosaria, and Marmae was now Sister Sheila. All were our first choices. We delighted in calling each other "Sister." The thrill of being addressed as Sister was probably much like a new bride when someone calls her "Mrs." the first time.

Just as we expected, our hair had to be cut completely to make room for the layers of fabric wrapped around our heads. The ceremonial cutting took place at the end of the day after our families had left. My expectations were of a short haircut, so I was prepared to see my straight brown hair go. I was not prepared for how short the cut would be and never expected to be bald.

Before Reception Day Sister Sheila asked Sister Philomene, "How long will it be?"

"It won't be," she replied.

The experience was especially painful for Ellen, who had gorgeous long, black hair, and Marmae, who had wavy, blonde ringlets. The clippers buzzed on and on, heard up and down the dormitory cubicles. It was a point of no return.

At evening recreation prior to reception of the habit, we practiced putting on the long, black leather belt—or girdle as it was called—a symbol of chastity. I caught on to that task easily thanks to the many saddles I had cinched on horses in my youth. Over the floor-length, black robe hung a scapular, a narrow black fabric, also to the floor. The scapular—a shoulder-to-shoulder fabric snapped together on one side over our scapula bones and fell straight down concealing any sign of a figure. We were taught to keep our hands under the scapular when walking.

Learning to wrap the coif around my face was the most difficult task to master. When laid flat, the starched and pleated fabric was pulled into the shape of a closed horseshoe. The pleats then had to be sewn together for stability. When dressing, we pulled two corners to the top of our heads, pinned them together, rolled the remaining unpleated ends of fabric from the top and pinned it down the back of our head to form the pleated platter shape under our chin. A white, starched linen triangle band wrapped around the forehead and folded to flatten into a Munster-like forehead. A short, white veil pinned to the stiff white band covered the folds and pins. The long, white veil falling over the shoulders and down the back completed the full habit. The daunting task ahead would be to get all of it on every morning by myself and get it straight.

Wearing the new habit was much like wearing a formal gown, with the exceptions of style and fabric. Our Sunday habit was made of heavy wool serge. The cotton one worn during the week was much cooler. We practiced walking up stairs without picking up our skirts; a necessity when carrying anything.

"The trick is to kick your heels out to the side, like this," Sister Philomene demonstrated on the stairs to second floor. "Swish your skirt out, that will leave room for you to step."

One by one, we practiced. The natural inclination was to pick up the skirts in front, but that's impossible while using both hands to carry books, buckets, trays, or anything.

"Not exactly graceful looking is it?" said Sister Sheila. After a few clumsy stumbles from stepping on our skirts and falling face forward, we mastered it.

I can't even explain how it felt to have my head wrapped up in layers. The coif had to be pulled to the top of my head so tightly that it left permanent indentations in my jawbone over time. Eating was a challenge. At first, we exaggerated the fork-to-mouth motion lest spaghetti land on the platter-shaped coif sticking out under our chin. A slow right angle up and over the coif, the way we made freshmen eat during initiation, worked. To avoid obstruction of side vision, the veil folds back when driving or working.

In many ways, the novice year was much like the postulant year with one major exception. For a full twelve months we were cloistered. We had little contact with anyone outside the enclosure. No more letters from home or visits from friends and family. Phone calls were never permitted. Parents were allowed to visit twice during the novice year. As novices we were expected to be even more aware of religious decorum and make every effort to grow in spirituality. No more singing Hank Williams "Jambalaya" or singing *anything* frivolous.

Putting on the habit and veil did result in a more sedate, holier-than-I-used-to-be feeling. Either the encumbrance of the habit and veil or the grace of God was working. Even the silence of each day became easier.

It might be a stretch to say I enjoyed the silence, but I learned to use it to develop an awareness of the presence of God in every moment. In silence, God can speak directly to us. This was true for me when outside absorbing the beauty of his world. All of nature in our limited surroundings was a wondrous testimony to God's love— from the smallest blade of grass to the brilliance of the sky. Daily distractions were limited in the peacefulness of silence.

Silence curtailed potential development of personality conflicts, anxieties, or pressures of jobs. With the abundance of quiet periods, there was little opportunity to share feelings; emotions were kept in check, which might have been good or bad. Life was peaceful and blissful. I found the quietness became a prelude to meditation. Though I didn't fully understand how to meditate, silence allowed an emptying of all superfluous thoughts making it easier to let God in. Gradually I got used to the aloneness felt while in the midst of many, but I never felt lonely. The few minutes of talking during the day were all the more joyous.

Every morning a half-hour period designated for meditation, followed Mass. I would spend my half hour reading a book about one saint or another for inspiration gleaned from their holy lives. Other than the general instruction to "contemplate God," I don't remember any "how to" methods of meditation taught. Eckhart Tolle's words would have been helpful back then. *When you practice meditative reading, you do not read to gather new information, but to enter a different state of consciousness as you read.* I wasn't aware of how to enter a "different state of consciousness," though I supposed that real contemplation must be something like that.

Contemplating sleep was much easier at that early hour. The thud of a book slipping from a lap divulged another nodding meditator. Once in a while, we could hear the heavy breathing of one of the older sisters catching a few winks. When the heavy breathing turned into snoring, front row postulants began snickering. I wondered how much real meditation was happening between the nods and the snores.

Chapter Twelve – *First Visit*

———

*D*aily routines differed little from year to year, though as novices, we made every effort to try to at least *look* more holy with our eyes cast down and hands under our scapular, shutting out all things secular. We were eager to greet new postulants when they arrived in the fall. They brought fresh news of life outside the convent. It was our duty as novices to introduce them to their new lives inside the convent. As the eldest-ranked novice, I was assigned to sleep in their dormitory on the third floor. I would have escaped that job and slept in the novice dorm if Lindy, now Sister Augustine, had not been held back, and therefore, dropped in rank. The third floor dorm felt more like an attic than a real dormitory; the windows were fewer and smaller. It was actually an extension of the dark adjoining attic room where luggage was stored. The single iron beds were placed side by side on each side of the room. The sterile dorm was the first test of religious life for any young girl fresh from her frilly, bright bedroom at home. My curtained cubicle was just inside the entrance to the room.

On a day like any other, the harsh clang of the antique school bell reverberated in the distant halls until it reached the doorway of the third floor dormitory. I suspected Sister Edmund, the bell ringer, *must* have slept in her habit to be dressed and ready to ring that bell before dawn. Her rumpled, thrown-together appearance suggested as much. Not known for her fastidiousness, her veil always fell a little cockeyed over what once was a precisely pleated white coif around her face.

I always loved being up in the early morning. I just never enjoyed *getting* up. At home, I would have hit the clock's snooze button, but now, there was no clock with a snooze alarm on the simple, wooden nightstand beside my narrow bed.

Miss Mary, one of the new postulants, flipped the light switch at the door and shattered the last spec of the night's serenity. As the only novice in the dorm, I should have been the one to rise quickly and turn on the lights as a model for the younger postulants. Procrastination is not an admirable trait in a nun. Habitual procrastination is tantamount to sin in a convent.

With reluctance, my feet hit the cold, hardwood floor one October morning. With knees bent down for a "Good Morning, God" prayer, I leaned against the bed, smothered my face in my hands, and turned prayerful thoughts to God. For an instant, I felt a strange feeling in my face.

Like a nest of birds fluttering their wings in the quiet of daybreak, the dormitory rustled with the movement of postulants dressing in morning silence. Sitting on the straight wooden chair next to my bed, I pulled on the black opaque stockings and rolled them down to just below the knees, giving them a twist into a knot. The long, straight, one-size-fits-all blue cotton slip slid over my head and narrow, young shoulders and fell almost to the floor. Modestly wrapped in my robe, toothbrush and toothpaste in hand, I drew back the white curtain around my cell and made my way to the common washroom just outside the dormitory.

My white towel and washcloth hung first in rank on the towel bar that stretched across the wall from corner to corner above the sinks. MAC initials stitched in red on the towel edges, appeared on all of my clothing for identification purposes in the laundry. In the land of anonymity, that simple mark displayed the rare evidence of personal possession. Those initials were a reminder of who I was before I became Sister Mary Magdalen.

Zombie-like, I moved around the washroom taking my turn at the sink. As I rubbed my face, I thought I felt a slight tightness on the left side of my face. The annoyance prompted a spontaneous urge to look in a mirror. There was no mirror, of course. The natural instinct was to study my face, more out of curiosity than vanity. Even if tempted, we had little to be vain about. Everyone wore the same clothing style, hair didn't show, and we never wore makeup. Regardless of the morning silence rule, I was tempted to ask Miss Carole, a postulant, to look at my face, but we needed to dress for chapel.

Piece by piece, I put on my habit, a ritual still new to me. On Reception Day, I had doubted I would ever get all eight pieces on straight and make it to the chapel in time for morning prayers. At least there was no time-consuming decision on what to wear.

I had all but forgotten my facial sensation through morning prayers, Mass, and meditation. No one gave me a strange look. Actually, no one looked at anyone. Gawking around was considered a distraction to our thoughts, as well as to others.

Sister Sheila and I were scheduled to serve breakfast to the sisters in the dining room. After Mass and before meditation, we left the chapel with the usual decorum. Once in the hall, we dashed down the stairs to the basement dining room to set up the table servings before the sisters came down to breakfast.

Breakfast was the easiest meal to serve, even while keeping the required silence. Sister Sheila and I had learned the system our first year as postulants. We could do it blindfolded. With sweeping, white veils tied back and long, bib-front, white aprons pinned on, we rushed around the institutional kitchen stacking toast on plates as it fell from the rotating toaster, pulling butter cubes from the walk-in cooler and placing them on serving plates. We passed white, cereal-filled bowls, cream pitchers, and jelly dishes to the tables. By the time the coffee pots were filled and ready for pouring, the other sisters filed silently down the stairs and lined up waiting for the signal to be seated at the long refectory tables in the painted white, cinder-block basement room. Everyone ate in silence as one of the sisters read from *The Lives of the Saints.*

After Sister Sheila and I finished clearing dishes, put food away, and cleaned up, we sat down to our breakfast. While washing the serving dishes in the long, shallow trough-like sink, I sensed the tightness again.

"Do you see anything wrong with my face?" I whispered to Sister Sheila.

With a quick glance and a shake of her head, she whispered, "No, nothing."

I put on a big smile and said, "Look again."

Silence was broken! "Oh, my gosh! Magdalen, what is wrong with you? One side of your face is frozen! You've got to go see Sister Bernarda." She pushed me off to see the nurse.

Sister Bernarda wore an all-white habit and veil. Her office was a three by five-foot dispensary, halfway down the second floor infirmary hall.

I waited my turn behind senior ranking sisters. Never an alarmist, Sister Bernarda spoke calmly, "Um hum, uh, smile again, dear."

She studied my face as she murmured reassurances. In my effort to smile again, I detected concern through her veiled calm. "What do you see?" I asked.

She handed me a mirror.

"What has happened to my face?" I gasped, begging her for an explanation.

The left side was totally paralyzed. There was no movement when I smiled.

Sister Bernarda rang Sister Philomene, and put in a call to the doctor for advice and an appointment.

"Until I hear from the doctor, I think it would be best for you to go back to the dormitory and rest. No more duties for you today."

I went to the dormitory and prepared for bed in the middle of the morning. I pulled the white curtains across the rods to enclose my little cubicle. Confused, frightened, and alarmed I fell asleep until Sister Sheila brought me lunch. After lunch, my fellow novices came to cheer me up. They made me laugh so they could see the half-frozen face. Although their silliness helped relieve my anxiety, they couldn't hide their sudden, shocked expressions.

The doctor prescribed vitamin B-complex shots and rest, but he gave no definitive diagnosis. At nineteen, I was too young for him to consider a stroke as the cause.

"It could be as simple as a draft on your face during the night, which would mean it is a temporary affliction," he said.

Even his ultimate assessment was tentative.

"From all indications and tests it might be Bell's palsy, a paralysis of the face, sometimes temporary, and sometimes permanent," he said.

That was enough to scare me into strictly following his orders. Bed rest in the isolated, third-floor dormitory felt like a punishment. I neither felt nor looked sick, at least not until I smiled. Fear of permanent paralysis began to set in. After a couple of days of restful sleep, I expected to see improvement. There was none, and as the second week began, I started to panic. The left side showed signs of drawing.

To occupy my time, I read the lives of the saints between frequent naps and visits from the nurse. If it had been permissible, I would have passed time writing letters. There was little to do but read, sleep, worry, and pray. Saying the prayers of the rosary occupied my mind. My fingers passed over the beads as I repeated a Hail Mary—at each bead, petitioning the Mother of God to intercede with her son on my behalf.

My anxiety increased as the next weekend approached. My parents were scheduled to make their first visit since Reception Day in June, the day I received the habit and became a novice. What if I was not back to normal by then? As eager as I was to see them, I didn't want them to be alarmed by my tragic-comic face. My father had already suffered two paralyzing strokes, and I didn't want the sight of my face to cause the third.

On the day of their visit, I had been dressed and ready since morning Mass at 6:30. When Sister Philomene came to announce their arrival, I walked slowly from the novitiate quarters down the wide, hardwood hall toward the large guest parlor, anticipating the fear I would see in my parents' eyes when they saw my face.

I made an effort to bounce into the room with some semblance of my usual joy. For a brief moment, I camouflaged the distortion in my face with tears of happiness at the first sight of them. They stood from the stiff, formal, Victorian parlor chairs to greet me with hugs. We had last been together in that room for pictures on the day I received my habit.

Though warned that I was not feeling well, they were devastated at the sight of the half-smile on my face. After a warm embrace, my dad held me back at arm's length to examine me. I caught the familiar scent of his cigar, a smell I normally disliked, but now it was a comforting smell of home. Mother was dressed in her Sunday best. As I hugged her, I could feel her posture slump. She bravely tried to maintain an upbeat conversation, but the cracking in her voice and the quiver of her lips betrayed her concern.

"Don't worry, Mom, I'll get better. It's probably only temporary."

"You can still eat, can't you?" My dad pulled a Mounds candy bar—dark chocolate no almonds—out of his jacket pocket, remembering the favorite bar he would always bring home to me when I was little.

They examined me over and over, hoping for my complete smile to show up. I suspected my father feared that I'd had a type of stroke. It was a natural first assumption because of his previous strokes and the history of heart conditions in his family.

Dad could look official and intimidating, standing tall and erect dressed in his Sunday three-piece suit instead of his farm work clothes. He pressed for an answer from Sister Philomene.

"What is being done to correct her condition?"

Sister Bernarda spoke up, "She is resting and taking shots prescribed by the doctor." In her calm nurse voice, she explained the Bell's palsy.

Her explanation was not sufficient for him. He was used to fixing things for me. Bowing to the nuns who were now in charge of my life crippled his take-charge style.

He grew quieter as the weekend progressed. I thought he must be regretting his decision to let me become a nun while still in my teens. I had been home from boarding school only three months before leaving again for the convent. He wanted me to wait at least a year to be sure of my decision.

We had a mutual admiration for each other, my father and I. He carried my baby picture in his wallet until the day he died and he granted my every wish for the pleasure of my smile. I knew I could always get what I wanted from him, but I was sensible enough not to push for the ridiculous. It hurt me now to see the anguish on his face.

At the end of the weekend, I walked them to their car and kissed them goodbye. The tears in my father's eyes conveyed his heavy heart. Mother struggled to smile as she said goodbye.

"Get your rest and follow the doctor's orders, Toots. I'll be praying hard."

I had no doubt that when my mother talked to God, he listened. I watched as they drove down the gravel driveway, turning toward home and the four-hour drive. My heart was breaking for them. I welcomed the isolation of bed rest as I pulled the curtains around my sparse cubicle and curled up in a tight ball.

I rested in the days and weeks that followed, eventually persuading Sister Bernarda that my energy was coming back. The alone time wore on me. I could do only so much reading, and I hadn't yet mastered the art of praying constantly. I often thought of home. I wondered how my parents were handling the lack of information.

With coaxing, Sister Bernarda allowed me to go to Mass and to meals, but I could not participate in any physical work activity. No cleaning, no dishes, no gardening, no serving at meals.

At my daily check-ins with Sister Bernarda, I got reports of gradual progress. My face seemed less drawn, and a slight crook of a smile showed. I was beginning to believe the paralysis might leave my face for good. Vitamin shots and prayers were working.

In early December, ten weeks after it struck me, the Bell's palsy paralysis was gone. By Christmas, I felt well again and back to normal. There were multiple reasons to celebrate. My parents' next visit was scheduled just after New Year's Day. They learned through Sister Philomene that the Bell's palsy was cleared.

As visiting day drew close, I anticipated a joyous reunion. After lunch that Sunday when Sister Philomene called me to the parlor, I wanted to run, but such behavior was not acceptable. I bounced into the parlor with joy in my heart and on both sides of my face.

I beamed the smile they had longed to see, "Merry Christmas and Happy New Year."

We chattered about everything. They shared news from home about my brothers, my girlfriend Linda's engagement, and my dog Mickey. They told me of their plans for a Florida trip in late January. Now that I was well, they felt they could go ahead as planned and take their first extended winter vacation to Ft. Myers Beach. My father's doctor had given him an all-clear sign at his recent checkup. They were looking forward to rest and relaxation.

I soaked up the smell of his cigar to remember until the next visit. When the evening prayer bell rang, it signaled time for them to leave and for me to go to chapel. We slowly walked arm in arm down the familiar hallway to the front door where I gave each of them a long, tight hug and wished them a great vacation. I saw a satisfied expression of contentment on my father's face. There were happy tears in the corners of his eyes. His little nun daughter was well.

Mother blew me a kiss from the car as they turned down the gravel driveway. At the last turn, my father looked back and gave me a smile and a final wave as he pulled out a cigar for the road.

He'd finally accepted that I was in good hands and happy with my life. He no longer needed to protect me.

Chapter Thirteen – *Loss*

―――

*J*ust four weeks after I saw them, my parents were enjoying several days in the Florida sun. On January 30th, after a morning at the beach, my dad walked to a nearby tourist store in search of cigars. As he headed back toward their beach cottage, he was stricken with a heart attack, collapsed, and died alone on the sidewalk of Ft. Myers Beach.

"Sister Philomene wants to see you," Sister Fabian said when she called me aside during that laundry day in January. It was an unusual request on a day when all hands were needed there. I didn't suspect anything was wrong because I couldn't think of anything I might have done to be in trouble. Visitors never came on a weekday, as a novice I wasn't allowed company except my parents, and they had just visited after Christmas before their vacation to Florida.

Back at her novitiate office, Sister Philomene sat me down on the little short-legged chair and gently broke the news.

"I have sad news, Sister. Your brother, Dick, called. You're father suffered a heart attack in Florida while they were on their vacation." She put a comforting arm around me.

"How bad is it?" He had recovered twice before.

"It was massive. He died in Ft. Myers Beach. Your brothers, Bill and David, are with your mother and Dick is on his way to pick you up. I am so sorry, Sister."

In no way could I comprehend what she had said. He'd had attacks before and recovered. He was only fifty-eight and had seemed so well when I saw him in December. I remembered our last goodbye and his contented smile knowing he was leaving me in the good hands of the nuns.

Driving home with my brother, I thought of my mother, alone without her life partner of thirty-two years. They spent years raising five children together, struggling through the Great Depression years, and barely saving their farm, only to lose nearly everything in the path of a ruthless tornado. They survived every challenge and made every decision together. Though she was a strong woman, I knew she would be lost without him.

I had not been in public since the day I received the habit. Returning home for the first time, I should have been jubilant. Instead, I felt sad, lonely, and awkward. When Dick and I arrived, lights were on all over the house. In the kitchen, women organized meals brought in by friends and neighbors, while men clustered on the porch and in various rooms, smoking and talking. The scene was a typical Irish wake. My mother wasn't home from Florida yet. She feared flying, so my oldest brother, Bill, was driving her home. Friends and family hugged me—most had not seen me as the little nun. Stumbling over what to call me, some were comfortable with Mary Ann. Others reverted to their Catholic training, respecting the robed, religious person, feeling they had to call me "Sister." I had never felt such awkwardness in my own home. I had only been gone a year and a half, but it was as though everything had changed—I had returned a different person. I was still a teenager fluctuating between needing to be a weeping little girl who lost her father, and struggling to be a pious, serious nun dressed up in black robes. I felt conflicted in trying to be what each person expected of me. I didn't even know what should be expected of a nun going home to family. I felt like a stranger in the house where I grew up, playing a role and unable to get my part right. I longed for my mother to be home so I could just be a daughter, not a nun.

It was long into the cold, winter night when the car pulled into the driveway. I rushed out to help Mom out of the car. The car lights exposed signs of exhaustion on her face from shock, grief, and the agonizing two-day drive. I put my arms around her to offer some comfort.

"I'm so sorry I couldn't bring him home to you, Toots," she said through her tears. She had such strength and compassion, always thinking of others, even in her deepest anguish. Enduring the sudden loss and the finality of never having her soul mate near again had to have been crushingly painful. She got little rest after the long ride from Florida; there were two days of visitation. Even the funeral stretched from the Decatur funeral home, to the funeral Mass at St. Michael's in Bement, to the burial in the Ivesdale cemetery. Seeing the sisters from St. Joseph School in Ivesdale at the cemetery comforted me. The burial was such a tearing of my heart.

Other than Linda, who was at my reception of the habit, my friends, mostly non-Catholics, had not seen me since I left home for the convent. The black garb was strange and weird to them. As anyone who returns home from experiences foreign to friends and family, nothing is quite the same, nor will it be. The commonality is missing. There were new experiences in my life to which no one could possibly relate.

In retrospect, I don't think I was much of a comfort to my mother. In my adolescence, I was more focused on how I felt than my mother's pain.

I was allowed a few days at home after the funeral to assist in whatever way I could. I tried to help by writing thank you notes and doing other tasks for Mother before I had to leave. One of the hardest things in my life was leaving her as she faced life without my dad. I couldn't imagine what it must have been like to lose half of oneself after thirty-two years. The harshness of convent rules that kept me from staying home with my mother at such a painful time was impossible to understand.

Without my father, she was left to make major farm management decisions they had once planned together. We both cried when I left to go back to the convent. Her four sons were close by, but her only daughter was cloistered in the convent, not allowed to communicate with the outside world, not even with her mother at the loneliest time of her life. Even though my brothers were steady pillars of support during the days and years that followed, I found it difficult to not be in contact with her, or even be able to write to her.

Never were the rules and restrictions of the convent more hurtful and harmful for me. A daughter should be at her mother's side when she's needed. I could not be. The archaic regulations of convent life never seemed more senseless. It was the mission of nuns to reach out to people in need. Some orders were established for that single purpose, but visiting our own families in need was forbidden at that time. After my father's death, the guilt of not being at home with my mother increased. Mother must have felt abandoned, yet she never complained about the rules that kept me away.

Six months were left in my novice year of training and striving for a more perfect life as God's servant. It would be the first of so many times over my years in the convent that I felt the burden of guilt for not being at home to do my share in helping my mother. She was a strong woman, but I should have been there to comfort her. I still carry the guilt, but whatever strength I have in times of trial, I got from her.

Chapter Fourteen –
First Vows and First Mission

⸻

*I*n the summer of 1955, profession of first vows was approaching. First vows are the same as final vows, with one major difference—first vows are promised for three years—final vows are for life.

The strict rules and seclusion of the novice year ease after completion of the twelve cloistered months required by Canon Law. Not until final vows, in three more years, would I be fully able to relax without the worry of scrutiny. After Lindy was held back, I felt no assurance of even being admitted to first vows. Final vows are a little like reaching tenure in teaching; once you reach it, you can't be fired.

Before acceptance into the community, a chapter meeting is held to evaluate each candidate. The many stories we'd heard of members being black-balled reminded us that acceptance was not a given until all members voted and we passed scrutiny.

"You don't really think any of us will be black-balled, do you? Wouldn't we be getting warnings by now?" Conversations on the possibility of rejection increased as profession day drew closer. None of us had broken any big rules. If not for the stunning decision to hold Lindy and Pat back from receiving the habit, we would have felt secure.

Evaluating us for vows was far more serious than when we received the habit. Voting decisions made by each final professed sister were based on her personal experience with the candidate and on recommendations from members who had known and observed the novice at work. Sister Philomene's reports carried the most weight.

Each professed sister was given two chips—one white and one black. After hearing the testimonials for each candidate, the sisters file past two boxes placed on a table in the center of the room. A chip is dropped in each box—one in a box for the vote, the other in the discard box. The number of white chips in the vote box determined acceptance of the novice for vows.

Helen, Sister Beatrice now, didn't wait for the scrutinizing vote at first vows. Midway through our novice year, she had gone back home. We had all been together for a year and a half. It was unsettling to learn of her decision. Once again, there were no goodbyes. Laundry day was always the exit day, a time when the person leaving could change into her secular clothes, and have her family pick her up without questions and goodbye tears from the rest of us. We learned of her departure at the end of the day, after she was gone. We never knew why she left. We assumed she decided the life was not for her, though we never saw it coming. There was little time to share feelings with one another. Those leaving were counseled by the superior and told not to tell anyone they were leaving.

Now we were five—Lindy and Pat completed their canonical year as novices in time to rejoin us for first vows.

The five of us waited in the novitiate for Sister Philomene to bring the results of the voting. Light conversation, nervous pacing betrayed our anxiety. The familiar quick footsteps approached through the adjoining community room. We held our breath. The smile on her face was enough to tell us the white chips fell in our favor. None of us were blackballed, or black-chipped. Sister Philomene must have felt a personal triumph; she had successfully transformed her first postulants from immature teenagers to women ready to make vows of stability to the Benedictine community. Though never good at showing spontaneous affection, a hug for each of us demonstrated her joy. We were all jubilant.

An eight-day retreat prepared us for the commitment we were about to make. We had studied the Benedictine vows of Stability, Conversion of Morals, and Obedience, during our novice year. Benedict's vows or promises, as he referred to them, pre-dated the traditional vows of poverty, chastity, and obedience by several centuries. All three Benedictine vows were intertwined, combining a full commitment to living a Benedictine life attached to a specific monastery. The promise of Stability was a lifelong commitment to God and to the monastery of entrance. Though sisters go out of the enclosure to do their work in service to the local people, they return to the monastery, often called the Motherhouse, where they have promised stability. The promise of Conversion of Morals signified a commitment to seek transformation to a life of holiness, including the simplicity of poverty and a life of chastity. Before promising a life of chastity, a young woman must be sure she is willing to give up marriage and having children. Classes on understanding the vows were meant to make sure we knew what we were about to promise.

Hundreds of communities, both men and women, not exclusively Benedictine, use the Rule of St. Benedict as their standard for living a community life, often modifying it to meet the needs of the times and their community. Benedict left room in the rule for adjustments based on needs. . . . *let the abbot make whatever arrangements suit best.* (Rule, Ch. 47)

Benedict instructed that everyone have the supplies needed, but he also wrote: *Let those who need more, ask.* (Rule, Ch. 55) In the novitiate, we each requested our supplies from Sister Philomene. In the community at large, a council member was assigned as a procurator. Sister Constance, the community procurator, charged with purchasing and distributing general supplies, as well as managing the entire facility, was a kindhearted soul who always looked worn out with the weight of her responsibilities. Her heavy frame moved from side to side down the hall as though trying to relieve first one tired foot, then the other. She managed her responsibilities with the wisdom and skill of an executive vice president.

We needed but to go to Sister Constance to ask for our basic supplies—everything from toothpaste to clothing. It was a humbling thing to have to ask for soap or toothpaste, but on the other hand, it was like having Dollar General down the hall without the need for a dollar. We didn't have our own money. Each time I knocked on the procurator's door to ask for simple toiletry necessities, it felt a little like begging.

Because Sister Constance had the weight of major convent decisions on her shoulders, I found it easier to ask Sister Martha, her assistant, for what I needed. She was as thin and wiry as Sister Constance was heavy and encumbered. Sister Martha always gave me something extra like a special soap.

"This is new, try it out," she would say like she needed my advice on a trial product. She and I referred to each other as our *special sister*—she was Martha, I was Mary of Magdala. She was the busy one taking care of others and the house; I was the non-domestic one preferring to sit in adoration of Jesus.

Sister Martha had a special direct line to Saint Joseph. In earlier community years of severe scarcity, when food was low, Sister Martha would put a bowl of a specific food behind St. Joseph's statue with a firm directive, "Joseph, we need this food to fill our pantry."

She addressed him as though he was right beside her. Joseph always responded to her requests. Sister Martha had an energizer-bunny zest in spite of multiple surgeries that left her with next to no stomach.

During the retreat, prior to making our first vows, Sister Philomene instructed us to practice writing the vows we would read at the ceremony. We wrote and rewrote them, read and reread them to ensure complete familiarity when reading in front of everyone at the altar. In practice, we processed to the altar, stood side by side across the wide sanctuary. Holding a mock-up copy of our vows, we practiced reading in unison, inserting our names one by one. A final, official copy was written on parchment paper which Sister Philomene kept until ceremony day.

We were privileged to be the first to make our profession of vows in the new convent and chapel, built during the course of our novice year. The old chapel was so small there was barely room enough for all the sisters. The new chapel was built to handle not only the sisters, but all students for Sunday Mass and guests during ceremonies. Three sections formed a cross. Down the nave, monastic style, upholstered, individual choir stalls with kneelers faced each side; a wide center aisle separated them. The cross wings of the chapel had blond wooden pews for guests and students. All wings faced the marble altar raised above a circular, rust-colored terrazzo floor. Behind the altar, a large crucifix, a German wood carving of the Risen Christ, hung in front of a magnificent black marble mosaic with gold and silver rays shimmering in the light. The flaming red of the sanctuary light, symbolizing the presence of Christ in the tabernacle, hung to one side before the mosaic. Stained glass windows in brilliant hues of blue, red, and gold reflected rainbow rays of sunshine into the chapel.

On our Profession Day, our families streamed into the guest wing. Everyone rose in unison as the organ announced the beginning of Mass and the entrance of all the Sisters—youngest to oldest—walking two by two, bowing to each other before taking their place in the teal blue, cushioned choir stalls. The solemnity of organ music combined with monastic ritual gave me a feeling of pride. The blessings of the Holy Spirit felt almost tangible.

We five novices,, wearing our white veils, were at the end of the procession right before Sister Philomene and Mother Mary Paul (newly elected Superior). We took the seats closest to the altar. At the Offertory of the Mass, Sister Philomene and Mother Mary Paul moved to the altar. Mother Mary Paul called us as a group for the reading of our vows. Carrying the official copy written on parchment paper and rolled diploma style, we took our places across the circular steps in front of the altar.

Mother Mary Paul asked, "What do you promise?" In unison, we read from the paper. Standing erect as my mother always taught me, I read loudly and clearly.

"According to the Rule of St. Benedict, and to the Sisters of St. Mary Priory, on this twenty-fourth day of August, 1955, I promise Stability, Conversion of Morals . . ." and then I stuttered. I bungled the next words. I wasn't in sync with the others. Startled, I couldn't figure out what had happened. Then I realized—in writing my final official copy of vows on the parchment paper, I had omitted the vow of Obedience.

I panicked. Unsure what it would mean I didn't know what to do. Would I have to do the ceremony again alone? Should I sign this copy now? I was the first to sign and didn't want to disrupt the ceremony, so I went up to the altar and signed the vow paper without promising obedience. Mother Mary Paul signed and sealed it.

The vow of obedience was an important part of my future life. Obedience was more than agreeing to accept a teaching assignment. It permeated every large and small detail of convent life—when to talk, when to eat, sleep, work, pray, what to wear, how to walk. How could I not have vowed obedience?

The omission distracted me from the solemnity of this major event in my life. The final step of profession was the pinning of the black veil. Feeling numb, I went through the motions as Mother Mary Paul and Sister Philomene placed the black veil on my head and slipped the white veil off. Removing the white veil meant we would no longer stand out in a sea of black. We were one with the other sisters, individuals but bonded in anonymity. The Mass continued. Sitting next to Sister Augustine we shared a nudge. My eyes met Sister Sheila's across the aisle. I still felt panicked at not promising obedience; I missed the euphoric feeling I might have had if all had gone smoothly.

Following Mass we processed out to the majestic organ music filling the nave and wings of the chapel. Greeted and congratulated by all our sisters, I could hardly wait to confess to Sister Philomene the omission of "obedience" in my vows, and learn how I could rectify it.

"We'll just get the vow paper and insert the word obedience where it should be. That will be just fine. Don't worry, Sister." But I did worry. I wondered if it was an omen.

Our families waited in the foyer to greet us with tears, hugs, and laughter. Mother and I shared a mixture of tears of happiness and sadness. We missed my father.

Once accepted and having professed our temporary vows, we would be considered Junior Sisters for the next three years. Still not permitted to mingle with or talk to the fully professed sisters, our recreation and meals were separate from them. That rule was relaxed if we were the lone junior sister assigned to a teaching mission with final professed sisters. Otherwise, we would never be able to talk to anyone except the superior, the pastor and the grade school children we taught. I heard that sometimes an over-zealous superior enforced the rule anyway, making it a miserable existence for the young teacher in a house with no one to talk to except the deluded superior.

My real test of living the vows began with the first assignment to a school. Adapting to life in a mission house could be easy or difficult, depending on the members in the house. Assignment Day was always in late August, a short time before schools opened. We never knew exactly which day. On the given day, the Prioress stood up at her place in the back of the chapel. Tension built. (During this period in the community history, the convent was called a Priory, the superior was the Prioress.) The Prioress gave a brief talk about the vow of obedience before reading the list of assignments she had no doubt worked on for weeks. I wondered if she had a big puzzle board in her office where she moved our lives around until every individual shape fit together. Sometimes assignments were determined after input from individual members, but not always. First-year junior sisters could not expect consultation. We were to accept our school assignment with blind obedience. Tension was evident in the exaggerated silence as everyone waited to hear their next mission, the grade they would teach, and who would be in their family group. It's like musical households. Each year you may live with different community members, at a different school, and in a new town.

Everything I had learned about obedience in the previous two years was about to be tested with my assignment to a mission school. And I hadn't even promised obedience. Mission by mission, the Prioress read the list. School first, superior-principal next, followed by the name of each sister and the grade she would teach.

"Sister Mary Magdalen, St. Peter and Paul's, Nauvoo, first and second grade."

"I will pray you don't teach first graders," words from my mother came back to me.

"What? Why?" I had asked.

"Because—you don't have the patience for them." Not exactly the vote of confidence I wanted from my mother.

St. Peter and Paul's was the local grade school in Nauvoo across the street from the Priory. At least I had escaped being sent out to a small town in a house with three people. I could live in the Priory dormitory.

As a junior sister, I still couldn't talk with professed sisters. On a mission, because there were few on staff, talking to everyone was accepted. At the Priory, we had to keep to ourselves at recreation and meal times. Lucky for me, Marmae—now Sister Sheila—was also assigned to a local school. Fresh from a year of cloister, with no practice teaching opportunity, we were thrust into classrooms. We hung out together that first year as we learned to teach. Sister Jane, a master primary teacher, taught us how to do lesson plans.

During the novitiate, we received college credits for Gregorian Chant and other courses that did little to prepare us for teaching. Education courses were limited to the few we received from Sister Rose. We received no courses on how to teach. It was sink or swim. That first year became my practice teaching. Many days I wasn't even treading water. I was sinking. I yelled entirely too much at those little tikes. My mother was right—she knew me. I thought I was prepared for the first day, but somehow I finished the lesson plans by noon, nothing to do then but stretch.

Years later when I met a couple of girls from that first class, I hugged them. They had grown into successful adults in spite of their primary education experience.

Mother Ricarda deserves credit for eventually setting up an off-campus center at the Priory, utilizing sisters qualified to teach courses necessary for a degree. Quincy College, Quincy, Illinois, and St. Ambrose College, Davenport, Iowa, agreed to the collaboration bestowing credits.

By the time of my third annual assignment day, my confidence level as a teacher had risen. I'd developed patience, and I could keep a classroom of wiggling little bodies under control.

While Mother Mary Paul read the long list of assignments, each sister sat motionless. Nervous anxiety showed on many faces awaiting their destiny. I glanced at Sister Sheila across the chapel holding her breath as well. We shared a grin.

I prayed for grace to accept the assignment, while at the same time, hoping to go back to Monmouth where I'd taught my second year. A compatible group of four, we lived in a lovely brick convent home next to the school. Sister Augustine (Lindy) and I were lucky enough to be together. My memories of that happy house were disrupted. Mother Mary Paul began announcing the Clinton, Illinois mission.

"Sister Mary Magdalen, Clinton, first and second grade." For a few moments I didn't hear another word of the assignments as I assimilated what Clinton meant to me. Whatever emotion sisters felt at their assignment—excitement, shock, sadness, or jubilation—no one expressed a sign of it in chapel.

I wanted to squeal with excitement. My home town, Bement, was thirty minutes from Clinton, another small rural farm community. The prospect of seeing my mother more often made me happy.

I began my third year of teaching and the final year of the Juniorate. Teaching had become more enjoyable than I expected. Juggling the forty little bodies with arms and legs in constant motion was definitely easier than my first year. I had accomplished the skill of teaching first graders on one side of the room, and second graders on the other, without yelling at any of them. I made my mother proud. If I succeeded this final year as a junior sister, I would receive final vows in the summer of '58. With final vows, I would be accepted into the community as a full-fledged professed member, committed for life.

Any thoughts of being sent home now were remote. Nor did I entertain any idea of leaving. My dream of being a fully accepted member of the community would be fulfilled. As it turned out, those were premature thoughts.

Chapter Fifteen – *Challenges*

A member of the parish in Clinton came to Nauvoo to pick up the four of us and deliver us to our new mission assignment. Since we had no car, we were indebted to the kindness of parishioners for transportation. Families in parishes were extremely generous. Often a woman of the parish would come to the house to cook our evening meal. Looking back, I wonder why we would have expected or allowed anyone to cook our meals. Those women had family schedules more demanding than ours. After the school day, our evenings were free to prepare classes, grade papers, enjoy a simple recreation, pray and retire.

The superior had the added responsibilities of house management and record keeping. Accepting the duties of being superior called for another blind obedience. Most sisters had no management training in personnel or in budgeting. Some handled the position better than others. The sudden responsibility thrust upon them came with the authority and power of leadership, but not necessarily the skills. An overzealous superior could take her responsibility too seriously, making life tense and even miserable for the other members.

Unlike Clinton and Monmouth, my first year of teaching at the local Nauvoo grade school was not a real mission experience. There were none of the usual duties of living with a small group. Living at the Priory, Sister Sheila and I had no cooking duties and few cleaning chores—our duty was to teach.

Clinton turned out to be a challenge for me. There were four of us, two of us barely twenty-one, another in her late fifties and the superior was around forty. Sister Michelle, the superior and seventh and eighth grade teacher, had been sent to nurses training to become an RN, but I don't remember her spending much time on the infirmary floor at the Priory. She must have preferred the classroom to nursing and got her wish.

St. John's three-story, brick grade school—surrounded by black top with not a blade of grass in sight—was not only our school, but also our convent home. Once in the door, I assessed and soon doubted how homey this venue would be. We carried our sparse luggage up three flights of wide, wooden stairs, every step echoing through the empty school. At the top of the stairs on the left, we could see the eighth-grade classroom. Across the hardwood hallway, we looked into an empty classroom with typical old-school, high ceilings, lots of windows, but no desks. Our voices echoed across the room, bounced off a couple of conference-type wood tables surrounded by straight-back chairs, struck the multiple windows, and boomeranged back.

"This is our recreation room," Sister Michelle announced with glee. I wondered if it was genuine enthusiasm or an attempt to keep us from panic at the sterile space. Already I was missing the homey neighborhood residence with carpet and soft, comfy furniture in Monmouth. I concluded that all missions were not the same. It crossed my mind that Clinton might be a test of my vocation before receiving final vows.

Double doors from the hallway led into our private quarters—a long, narrow hall across the back of the third floor with tiny, private windowless bedrooms. At one end, the hall opened into a dining room attached to a room-for-one-cook kitchen. Except for the presence of

Jesus in a chapel near the dining room, there was little warmth. Sterile, chilling, and institutional were the words that came to mind.

Sister Michelle, my superior, fit into the sterile atmosphere. Her personality lacked softness; squinted eyes behind round, thick, magnifying eyeglasses gave her a Peter Lorre look. She must have been uncomfortable as our superior; we were not a mix of easily compatible companions. My carefree Irish personality may have annoyed Sister Michelle's efficient German intensity. Sister Sylvester was a short, round, bundle of joy—a music teacher and a poet—living happily in her own world of writing jingles for contests. Sister Pat was a tense, quiet soul still fighting her own internal battles—maybe left over from having been detained as a postulant.

Looking back, there could have been only one explanation for putting the four of us together, rattling around in the isolated upper quarters of an empty school. Mother Mary Paul must have gotten to the end of assignments on her big checkerboard, taken the leftovers, and squeezed them into Clinton. Sister Michelle might have felt that way too. If consulted, we couldn't have been her first choice companions.

With little to no cooking experience, I took my turn at routine meal preparation. A duty poised for disaster. Life in a boarding school deprived me of the benefits of learning at my mother's side in the family kitchen. During summers at home from school, learning to cook was the last thing on my mind.

I always figured if I could read, I could cook. The day I tried to bake biscuits from scratch proved me wrong. Recipes are written with the assumption that you know your way around a kitchen. Calling my mother was out of the question. How hard could it be, a little flour, a little water, and I'd serve up delicious biscuits. Somehow two clumps of dough became stuck to my hands—none of it on the kneading board as the recipe suggested. I knew what it meant to "knead the dough," but *how do I knead it when it's stuck to my hands?* I wondered.

Mother would not have been proud, but she would have seen the humor in the Lucille Ball comedic scene.

The humor of the situation was lost on my superior. I felt her displeasure at my ineptness. The biscuits were not fit for consumption. A silent meal was a blessing this once. Making small talk through the tears would have been painful. I was a failure as a cook. On other missions, I might have suffered through a few jokes about my baking skills, but it was painfully *not* funny this time.

Other fiascos that year shook my confidence in my ability to have what it takes to be a good nun. Cooking was the least of it.

"Sister, I shrunk the new altar cloth," I confessed, kneeling before Sister Michelle.

I was in charge of being sacristan at the parish church. My duties consisted of preparing the altar linens for Mass and filling the cruets with wine and water every morning. Altar linens were to be washed, pressed, and folded each week, then placed in cabinet drawers in the sacristy room near the altar. Sister Michelle had instructed me to wash the newest altar cloth before using it on the altar, which I did. I thought it seemed a bit shorter after washing it. I was right. It no longer reached the floor on each side of the altar as intended. Washing linen in the wrong water temperature can have disastrous results— another thing I never learned at home. No amount of ironing would successfully stretch it. Kneeling for a penance became a frequent occurrence that year.

I loved teaching more and more. I found nothing as satisfying as the challenge and ultimate accomplishments of moving first and second graders along in their primary education.

How could I forget sweet Agnes who proudly contributed her stamps from home to the classroom cancelled stamp collection? I noticed that one of her more colorful stamps stood out. I rescued it from the barrel of stamps to look at it closely.

"Agnes, this is a beautiful stamp. Does your mother know you brought this one to school?"

"No, Sister, I found it in a box. So I put it with the others I brought."

"It is so nice, Agnes, you might want to take this one back to your mother before we put it in with all the rest. See what she says."

The prized, first-issue, wedding commemorative stamp from Princess Grace and Prince Rainier's wedding in Monaco was no doubt a keepsake. One not to be dumped in the pile of cancelled stamps collected at school.

I still remember angelic Maureen, who snuggled up to me at my desk after her first confession made before making her first communion.

"Sister, I forgot one part," she whispered.

"What part was that, Maureen?"

"The part that comes after 'Bless me, Father, for I have sinned.'" Of course she had forgotten it; that sweet angel had no sins to remember.

Teaching in Clinton had a plus side—it was easier for my family to visit from Bement, only a few miles away. After the austerity of the novice year, visitors were again allowed once a month. Linda came one Sunday with my mother. Visiting in that bleak recreation room, sitting on straight wooden chairs, gave me an uncomfortable feeling. The contrast to my mother's home, plush with carpeting and cushioned furniture was obvious. It hardly seemed like a way to welcome guests. I couldn't help thinking Linda, a newly married lady, looked far more mature and aware of the world than I felt. I hadn't seen her since she came to my reception when I received the habit. Our lives had gone in separate directions. I missed being her maid-of-honor when she married during my novice year. I could not have been *in* her wedding anyway. The Church did not allow Catholics to participate in a non-Catholic's wedding at that time. That would have been a heart breaker.

We seldom communicated during those early years when we were each building new lives.

I survived the year in Clinton, but after spending five years of my life toward reaching final vows, my confidence in being accepted was shaken. I had lingering doubts that Sister Michelle would recommend me as a viable candidate.

"Do you think you are ready for final vows?" The question during one of our conferences stunned me. She made it clear to me that she didn't think I was ready. She conveyed that assessment to Mother Mary Paul.

Sister Michelle's recommendation was critical. Only she could testify to my success or lack of it that final year of the Juniorate. The number of white chips of acceptance or black chips for rejection that I would receive that summer at the chapter meeting hung on her words. At the end of the school term, I wondered if I would be taking my black trunk back to the same school, a new school, or home to Mother. The possible scenario was tantamount to finishing the last semester of college and calling home to say, "Don't come for graduation, I failed."

Chapter Sixteen – *Final Scrutinium*

Scrutinium, the dreaded evaluation process held prior to acceptance for final vows, was upon us. As candidates, we were required to go before the entire community, kneel in the center of the rows of sisters seated in the community room, and humbly ask to receive final vows and acceptance into the community for life.

The five of us waited in the hall to be called into the meeting. "After five years, surely they won't vote us out now," I suggested to the others, not at all sure of my own confidence.

"It's been done before," said Lindy. The tension in her face reflected the dread that had haunted her at every evaluation since our postulant year when she had been held back from reception of the habit.

Sister Clarisse called us in.

"Don't be nervous," she said.

How could we not be nervous? All eyes were on us as we walked into the room. It felt like a trip to the guillotine. We knelt before them, gathered our gumption, and said our piece in unison asking to be admitted to final vows in the Benedictine community of St. Mary Priory.

We rose, our hands under our scapulars, eyes lowered, and left the silent assembly to assess our fate. Five years of trying to become a good nun came down to a decision over which I had no control. Ultimately, the community's discernment would decide my fate.

They would discuss each of us while we waited. Sister Clarisse, our supervisor for the three years we were in first vows, had given testimony. I felt reasonably confident she would give all of us a favorable report. Our superiors from missions, plus any of the other sisters who felt they had something significant to report about us— either positive or negative—could weigh in. The scrutiny could last for hours, much longer than for first vows. They discussed our conformity to the vows, our health, our character, our ability to get along with others, and who knows what else.

We were not only committing ourselves to *them*, the community was committing to *us* for the rest of our lives—to feed, to clothe, educate us—to care for us in sickness and in health, until death.

All we could do was pray at that point. We divided our time between the chapel and pacing the floor in the annex room. Several hours passed before Sister Clarisse came out of the community meeting with the results. She was smiling, a good sign.

"You all passed scrutinium; you are accepted to receive your final vows," she said. Spontaneous hugs all around showed our happiness and relief.

Though I passed, I couldn't help but wonder how my year in Clinton with Sister Michelle might have affected the number of black chips I received. Superiors from all three of my assignments would have reported on my readiness for vows, but it was her testimony that worried me. She had made it clear to me and to Mother Mary Paul that she doubted my vocation. The thought that I may have barely made it was unsettling. Strict secrecy is held regarding all reports in scrutinium. It is a strange feeling to walk among the sisters after such an event, wondering what they heard and what they were thinking. I put the tentative feeling behind me and prepared for my profession of final vows—lifetime vows. I had been accepted, that was all that mattered.

Family and friends were invited to witness the solemnity of this major milestone in my life. I had just turned twenty-three and I was about to take the final step of consecration to seeking God as a Benedictine sister, and vowing stability to the Nauvoo community forever.

The most significant and dramatic ritual of the Final Profession Ceremony, *going under the pall,* left a stirring impression. The funeral pall, a heavy black cloth, large enough when unfolded, spread over all five of our prostrate figures stretched out on the cold, terrazzo floor in front of the altar. Going under the pall symbolized our *death to the world.* We would continue to be *in* the world, but no longer *of* the world. We were to "put aside the world's temptations forever." In that solemn, dramatic moment, I experienced an awesome, grace-filled feeling. A magical transformation was taking place. I felt as though I would rise from under the dark pall as a new person, free from all worldly temptations, expectant that growth in holiness would come easier with this final consecration to God. As if going under the pall were not symbolic enough of our death to the world, we wore a crown of thorns as Jesus had done at his death, in contrast to the floral wreath worn at the reception of the habit.

The original vows written on parchment paper at our first profession were brought out of the archives to be read and signed once again. Standing before the altar, each of us holding the vows we had written three years before, we read them in unison—promising Stability, Conversion of Morals, and Obedience. This time I did promise obedience. I read the shaky handwritten word "obedience" squeezed in at a slant between words, the way I had written it three years before. It looked as though I promised obedience as an afterthought. I smiled to myself at the possible truth in that thought. The prized moment of the ceremony came when we received the gold ring inscribed with bold black IHS letters, the symbol of Christ. Mother Mary Paul handed me the ring, the priest blessed it, and I put it on my finger. It signified my commitment to God and to the community. My life as a professed Sister could proceed. I had what was tantamount to tenure.

Year after year, I had pulled out my little footlocker trunk ready to travel at the end of each school term. On each mission, I packed my clothes, teaching supplies, everything I owned in the trunk, except for clothes I needed for the summer. I taped a piece of typing paper with my name written in bold, black letters on the lid of the trunk. The address space was blank because I never knew where I would be sent to teach until assignment day in August. The trunk had to be prepared for shipping in the event we did not return to the same mission. I spent several years moving from one mission to another across the State of Illinois. Some sisters taught in the same place for several years, I seldom returned for a second. It concerned me, but one of my friends put my wonder at ease, suggesting that my congenial nature allowed me to fit in anywhere and with most anyone.

During those years of moving from one mission to another, I missed two family weddings and the birth of four nieces and a nephew. My brother Bill, widowed, married a lovely woman named Lois; they had two girls and a boy. I'll never forget when I received word of my first niece's birth, little red-haired Janet. I was teaching in LaSalle, Illinois, and excited to be an aunt again. Dick and Pat had two girls and a boy. I first saw their youngest, Carrie, when I attended summer school at the University of Illinois in Champaign-Urbana. Both families lived in Bement. Mother often sent pictures.

I'll never forget one particular Sunday when the mission assignments were read in Chapel. The Prioress, as usual, read through all assignments to schools. When she completed the mission list, my name had not been mentioned. I couldn't imagine I missed it.

I leaned to Sister Augustine and whispered, "Did you hear my name?" A negative response; her eyebrows raised, her shoulders shrugged in question. Once again thoughts of insecurity gripped me. I had my ring, I had made final profession. *Where are they putting me now?* I wondered.

The Prioress continued. "Assignments to college: Marycrest College, Davenport, Iowa—Sister Rosaria, Sister Mary Magdalen." I was assigned to a year of study on the college campus—a totally unexpected surprise.

Typically, we received our college education attending summer schools year after year at various colleges because our community had no affiliate college. I was teaching long before receiving my degree in education, and long before I knew how to teach. In those days, the practice was not singular to convents. From the days of *Little House on the Prairie*, well into the fifties, many young women taught school without a full teaching degree. An assignment to a full year of study on a college campus was rare for our community. Only one or two sisters a year received the privilege.

I looked across at Sister Rosaria (Miss Ellen). Her surprised expression mirrored mine. My next thought was *what will I study?"* I was almost certain Sister Rosaria would be in music. I had gotten vibes in the past that they might want me to teach music—only because I could sing. I assumed they thought better of it after reprimanding me for singing Hank Williams songs.

At breakfast Sister Rosaria and I exploded with excitement, trying not to be too exuberant lest we irritate other sisters who had plugged away at their education summer by summer. Though some must have felt overlooked, they expressed genuine happiness for us.

"You'll be studying music, don't you think?" I suggested to Rosaria. "And I'm hoping I might study secondary business education. What else would it be? They wouldn't need to fast-track me in elementary education."

It wasn't unheard of that a sister would be assigned to study in a field she wouldn't have pursued by choice. Obediently, she would have to follow the directive of the superior to fill a need in the community. That might have been Sister Michelle's experience when she received her RN.

When we were finally told, I felt blessed to be chosen to study in the field of business, my preference since high school when I had admired my mentor, Sister Joann, who taught me all my business classes. Maybe my dad looked down and gave me this wish. Sister Rosaria would major in music, just as she hoped.

As much as I enjoyed the primary grades, spending the rest of my life teaching six and-seven-year-olds would have required a large helping of grace and a mother's prayers to supplement my patience. With business training, I hoped one day to return to my *alma mater* to teach. That would fulfill the vision I had held since entering the community.

Marycrest College, a Catholic women's college in Davenport, Iowa, founded by the Sisters of Humility, had an excellent academic reputation. At Marycrest, I experienced teachers who were dedicated to empowering women through excellence in education. It was my first introduction to the concept of empowerment for women religious in the world.

Sister Rosaria and I shared a room. I became friends with Yogamani Leo of Ceylon, a student interested in the life of a nun in the States. She accompanied me to Nauvoo one weekend where she found our prayer life inspiring. The welcoming spirit of the sisters impressed her. *All guests who present themselves are to be welcomed as Christ, for he himself will say: I was a stranger and you welcomed me* (Matthew 25:35, Rule, Chap. 53)

At Marycrest, I began to whet my appetite for all things business related, an interest first developed in my high school business classes. I relished the college courses in investments though it would have little practical application for me. It was not likely that I would ever develop my own portfolio or become the community treasurer.

Graduation day at Marycrest was as thrilling for my mother as for me. I was the first college graduate in the family. Proud of my accomplishment, I still knew that a diploma didn't make me any smarter than my older brothers who were all accomplished in farm management.

After I received my B.S. in Business Education, the assignment I dreamed of—teaching at the Academy where I had grown up— became a reality. Sister Rosaria took the choir director and music teacher positions. Sister Sheila (Marmae), who had a year of college before she entered, finished her degree in Home Economics and headed that department. Three out of five of us were together and back at the Academy—unbelievable. Sister Joann took the place of Sister Rose as principal, another stroke of luck for me. It hadn't occurred to me while studying business that I could end up teaching on a faculty under Sister Rose as principal. That would have been my Waterloo since she never exactly favored me. With Sister Joann's assignment as principal, I filled the need for a business teacher to take over her teaching duties. Sister Estelle, head of the business department, mentored me. My students were barely twelve years younger than I, but at least I was better prepared for teaching business than I had been for teaching first grade. The Academy was more than my *alma mater*; it was the foundation of my youth. I loved every moment of fulfilling my vocation at the school that was dear to me in so many ways.

Assigned as freshmen prefect in St. Joe's Hall, the dormitory where I lived as a sophomore felt like déjà vu. In ten years, nothing had changed. Each floor housed approximately twenty-five girls. Single iron beds lined up barracks-style along the walls and down the center of the room. A small, one-drawer nightstand with a mirror and a wooden bench with a lift-top seat where white bobby socks were stored in neat rows, stood between each bed. At the foot of the bed was the same type three-drawer brown stand I used as a freshman in North Dorm.

As a prefect, my private sleeping space consisted of a 6' x 8' space at one end of the communal shower room beyond the dormitory. It was tantamount to sleeping in a bathroom. I had a twin bed and a small dresser—the simple necessities of convent life. A heavy curtain drawn at the foot of the bed separated my space from the shower room. In retrospect, I must have aspired to that prefect job rather than another Academy duty simply because I wanted to follow in the footsteps of Sister Joann, who had been my prefect in the same dorm. Why else would I have considered it a plum job to sleep in a bathroom only ten feet from sleeping teenagers.

As a prefect and teacher, every moment of my life was devoted to the students, teaching them, recreating with them, and living with them in the dorm. After monitoring an evening study hour in a classroom, I returned with them to the dorm where "lights out" was at 10 p.m. Just as my teachers had done before me, I became the teacher, counselor, friend, and proxy-mother for girls who left their homes and came to St. Mary's for a Catholic education. In those first years of teaching and prefecting in St. Joe Hall, I built a catalog of favorite memories.

After a couple of years, I moved upstairs to the sophomore dorm. One night after study hour, I reached the top of the stairs with several girls following me. Opening the door, I switched on the overhead florescent lights and found a bat flying frantically around the room above rows of beds. Slamming the door, I kept the girls out in the hall. I pulled Betty—a brave student who volunteered—in with me. With my skirts tucked up, veil pulled back and both of us armed with brooms, we swatted at the bat between muffled screams and laughter. Adrenalin was pumping. We had to do something fast before the gang in the hall began clamoring to get in and set off a riot of screaming teens.

Somewhere in my memory of practical gems from country living, I remembered that if a bat is grounded, it cannot fly. To fly, it must launch itself from a tree or someplace above ground. After the flying bat narrowly missed my veiled head and Betty's hair yet again, a swing of the broom connected and we grounded it. Gingerly scooping it up in a dustpan, we sent it back to its nocturnal environment through a window. Though my heart was pounding when I let the girls in, I needed to remain calm to keep them from being awake all night with visions of bats flying above them. I, on the other hand, slept with the covers tucked over my head all night.

Those were the "good old days." I was happy teaching my favorite subjects, students were happy, and the Academy was thriving with an excellent faculty. We enjoyed great camaraderie.

The school was famous for putting on plays, mostly for the student body, sometimes for the locals. A taste of the arts was an outlet for the girls' dramatic side. The costume room for all those plays was in the back room of the second floor of St. Joe Hall where Sister Stephen and I were prefects. Boxes and boxes were filled with outfits any costume designer could use to transform an ordinary schoolgirl into a Victorian lady, a Gilbert and Sullivan sailor, a Shakespearean villain, a Grecian goddess, or a 1930s flapper.

One summer day before the beginning of school, Sister Stephen and I felt like celebrating on a feast day—a day of talking. We decided to entertain some of the faculty members relaxing on break in the faculty room at the Academy. Rooting through the boxes marked "hats," "jewelry," "dresses," we donned the finest hats, beads, and shawls—any colorful finery that would fit over our veils and habits.

The faculty sisters seated at the long conference table were having a Coke break from an afternoon of work. With aprons on, veils folded back, and sleeves rolled up from cleaning, they were enjoying the frivolity of a feast day.

Sister Stephen and I caught them off guard. We sashayed in twirling our necklace beads. Sister Stephen bubbled with laughter in her bright orange, cap-sleeved dress as her feathered hat bobbed over her ruddy, cute face. My Kentucky Derby style, wide-brimmed, black hat with a flourish of poppy flowers topped my 1920s purple dress and bauble beads. An explosion of laughter erupted.

The walls of that old, tiny, faculty room had witnessed lots of merriment, tears, and probably some gnashing of teeth. I had heard stories of the days when Sister Rose was principal. The volume of frivolity would drop a few decibels as her heavy footsteps approached. Faculty members in those days were not exempt from the terror of her bulletin board postings.

As much as we hated to see the old school come down after seventy years—demolishing memories of good times—deterioration of the building and growth of the enrollment dictated the need for a new classroom building with better lab facilities and library. In addition to the school, a three-story dorm was built to accommodate freshmen and sophomores.

The usual routine of cleaning rooms on Saturday before leaving the dorm continued in the new Mary Hall dorm. The new building provided more privacy for the girls with two to a room rather than living in an open dorm with twenty girls. I had the luxury of a private room with connecting bath. Monitoring the students behind closed doors was more difficult, but they deserved privacy. While late night cigarette smoke was no doubt blown out the windows, the lingering smell of smoke in the room was a giveaway that someone had broken the "no-smoking" rule. Saturday morning chores were just that—a chore, for some more than others. Sheets needed to be changed, drawers cleaned and organized, hair washed, and rooms cleaned. The checklist of duties was still in effect just as it had been in my freshmen year and the excessive cleaning was still considered an unnecessary burden by the less domestic.

One morning, Bonnie, a senior, was ranting to her roommate, "I am not going to clean up this shit and if Maggie wants it cleaned, she can clean up the shit herself."

She must have thought I was miles away. Overhearing her, I wandered down the hall and into their room, "How are you doing with your cleaning, girls?"

"Just fine, Sister," said Bonnie.

"Oh, I just wondered. I thought it might be a mess with all that shit flyin' around."

I made a quiet exit. First silence, then stifled giggles, then a cleaned room.

Chapter Seventeen –
Effects of Vatican II

*I*n the early days of Catholic institutions in America, selected
women in religious communities studied finance, administration,
philosophy, and business—the secular subjects necessary to run
educational, hospital, and other institutional facilities. Sister
Constance, procurator, Sister Fabian, treasurer, Sister Rose, and Sister
Ricarda were among the women in our community who had received
higher education. They became leaders of the institution.

Educated women in convents were among the first liberated
women. They founded schools of higher education, built the largest
private school system, and nonprofit hospital systems in the country.
As John J. Fialka wrote in his 2003 book, *Sisters: Catholic Nuns and
the Making of America,* "They were the nation's first large network of
female professionals in an age when the pervading sentiment was a
woman's place was in the home."

Nuns staffed thousands of private schools serving the educational
needs of millions. The church grew on the backs of the women of
religious orders. Sisters served in dioceses from coast to coast under
the jurisdiction of priests, bishops, and archbishops, who treated
them as chattel, controlling their community elections, finances, and

assignments. As far back as the fourth century, men even determined the manner of dress nuns wore.

Few nuns sought to question the centuries-old, religious customs brought from Europe. The common practice was to leave their convents by day to teach, return to the convent after the workday, and remain behind closed doors. The outside world was not invited inside the cloistered part of the building. *Great care and concern are to be shown in receiving poor people and pilgrims...*; (Rule, Ch. 53) As in Benedict's day, guests were welcomed and served in a separate dining room equipped with fine china and sterling. Though I never found it, I suspected my Lily of the Valley pattern silver was serving guests.

It is no wonder the world considered us a mysterious bunch—robed in black, never looking up, seen only in twos when outside the convent. Many parishioners whose origins were European accepted the mystery as religious piety, though they knew little of our life behind the walls. They must have felt the presence of the "good sisters" was some kind of blessing—like the blessing parents felt when a daughter or son entered religious life.

European sisters who came to America eventually relaxed their ancient cloistered rules, adapting to the necessities required by their missionary work of caring for the sick, educating children, and defending against injustices. In the early twentieth century, many women joined convents to experience an adventure that would take them out of the realm of housewife and into service. My own decision to enter was similar.

In the early nineteen sixties, my myopic vision kept me from seeing what became clear in hindsight—the world was changing outside our walls. Convents across the country were feeling the effects of the changing role of women in secular society. Women entered college in increasing numbers to study for degrees more varied than traditional teaching or nursing. Realizing opportunities for new roles in the workforce, more women sought education leading to professional positions normally relegated to men.

Liberation for women was beginning.

Nuns inside convent walls were searching for new ways to fulfill their religious vocation. They were awakened to the needs in society—needs neglected by many religious communities. It didn't make sense anymore to lead insulated lives of prayer and teaching, while practicing minimal acknowledgement of, and influence on, the world outside. Some were ready to break out of the confines of convent walls, not necessarily to abandon the vow of stability, but to have the freedom to live the life of the Gospels—to choose work that would help the poor, the deprived, and those discriminated against.

Young women choosing convent life looked at it not only as a calling, but also a career. They were different from the "Hail Mary" girls of the previous decade—my decade. They had experienced more freedom, more independence, and more intellectual curiosity. Questioning long outdated community rules—whether verbally or mentally—came naturally to them. The changes were becoming unsettling to some of the sisters, both young and old.

Our parishioners also found the growing unrest in religious communities disturbing. With good reason, it turned out. Though there was no single reason, the changing roles of nuns resulted in the closing of many schools in small town parishes. School closings were also brought about by social changes and consolidation of large public schools offering broad curriculums and popular social outlets for young people. No longer did children prefer to be taught by the good sisters, and no longer did parents consider religious education a priority.

Sister Martha, way ahead of her time, always reached out to people in need even before the birth of the outreach movement. She was a regular visitor at the Iowa State Penitentiary in Ft. Madison, Iowa, just across the river from Nauvoo.

One evening after supper, she stopped me in the hall. I noted a twinkle in her eye and a hint of a smile on her lips. Something was on her mind and I could tell I was about to be included.

"My Sister," she said. "I have a question for you." Whatever the question, I was prepared to do anything for her.

"My guy at the prison has a buddy who would like a sister to visit him or write to him. Would you be interested in doing that charitable work for God?" she asked.

I didn't need to think about it. "Sure, I would like to. Would I go with you?"

"At first you can, but we wouldn't always be able to go together."

On my first visit, I stuck close to Sister Martha and followed her lead. Prison guards are tough-looking and have a no-nonsense demeanor. The entry formality was sobering. I could have hidden any number of breakout tools in the folds of my garb, but giving us the benefit of any doubt, we weren't frisked, though, I felt frisked by the up and down stare of the guard.

A guard searched my purse and deposited it in a small locker. The echo of clanging iron gates closing behind me as I entered the first enclosure took my breath away. I was trapped in a cage with the escape route behind me and the unknown ahead of me. The visiting room was surprisingly amicable. Inmates and their visitors were chatting at several tables and chairs. Guards stood at attention on each side of the room. Expecting to talk through a hole in a window or with a phone, I found the visiting arrangement quite casual. I wasn't sure I wanted to be that up close and personal with a prisoner—a man I had never met—sitting across from me at a table no bigger than a card table. I knew nothing of this man or his crime. I could tell he scrubbed and polished from head to toe for the visit. His face was shiny clean, dark hair slicked back; he wore a white shirt and blue pants, both looking prison pressed.

Harley was in his mid-thirties, tall and thin, educated, and an accomplished musician. Somewhere in his youth, he had made a bad choice resulting in multiple incarcerations. I began visiting him once a month; we wrote letters between visits. He had many questions about my life but told me little of his. I didn't pry.

"A robbery went very wrong when I was young," he said, sharing no further explanation. He preferred to talk about his music; he was a classical guitarist, as well as accomplished on the saxophone. No family or friends visited him. He was extremely grateful to have someone from the outside to visit with, someone to share his interest in music.

"Do you know *The Girl from Ipanema*?"

"I'm not sure. I don't recognize the title." I hadn't kept up on popular music.

He hummed a few bars of a current favorite; I recognized it, not because I knew it by title, but because I had heard it playing on the radios in the girls' dorm.

"Do you have any favorite songs?" he asked. I could only think of some show tunes from *Sound of Music* and *My Fair Lady* that I liked.

I suppose Harley was the beginning of my outreach awareness. During following visits he talked about the talent show the inmates put on every year.

"Do you think you could come to it?"

"Love to," I said, "I'll check with Sister Martha to see if we can come together." I knew I couldn't attend a prison concert alone, nor did I want to. I figured Sister Martha would be more likely to get permission for us to attend.

Harley reserved us the best seats—front and center—in the prison auditorium. The audience of local people, prison personnel, and a few families of the inmates filled the large venue. The talent hidden away behind those bars was astounding. A complete orchestra of tuxedo-wearing inmates opened the show, followed by individual acts, instrumental and vocal. Harley's classical guitar solo would make you weep. The band played *The Girl from Ipanema*, featuring Harley on his sax. Lost in the musical moment, we could have been at any concert until brought back to reality at the finale, when armed guards escorted us out of the auditorium without an opportunity to congratulate the performers. Harley had spotted us in the audience and gave us a big smile. Though I had never known him before, I felt we were friends.

On one of my visits later, I asked him if he felt the prison warden would permit me to bring in a group from our senior girls' choir from the Academy to do a concert on their stage. He was thrilled with the idea and pursued plans to make it happen. I got permission from the principal and he received permission from the prison administration. The girls were excited on the bus ride to the prison, though a little scared at the strict ritual at the entrance.

Guards led us single file to the auditorium. Harley was there— all smiles to see us. He managed the technicalities of arranging to have a piano and risers on the stage. He must have been a trusted inmate because he was given freedom to be backstage with me during the concert. Guards were everywhere, so I had no anxiety. I trusted Harley, but felt a heavy responsibility for the girls with all the other inmates around. The girls, of course, were a big hit. They found it a bit intimidating when the stage curtain opened and they saw the auditorium filled with inmates all eagerly hooting, hollering, and whistling as they anticipated the show.

It felt good to bring a little outside exposure into their imprisoned lives. When I visited Harley next, he was so happy that we succeeded in pulling off the concert. I was also pleased and relieved that it went well. I continued to visit him until I was transferred to another school away from Nauvoo.

While society in the nineteen sixties was slowly opening its mind to the expanding role of women, the Catholic Church continued to see nuns as subservient to Church authority. The Bishop of Peoria, Illinois, considered the sisters of St. Mary's Monastery in Nauvoo, as belonging to his diocese. After his death, the sisters voted overwhelmingly to become a pontifical community, giving the community independence from any local bishop. I was still a Junior sister in temporary vows at the time and the impact of this went over my head. As a Junior sister, I was not included in the chapter (professed sisters only) meetings. I didn't fully understand the impact of being a pontifical community, though the idea of independence from the hierarchy of bishops and priests was not difficult to understand or embrace. To solidify our independent strength, the community applied to and was accepted into the Congregation of St. Benedict—a group of independent Benedictine community motherhouses. The affiliation afforded better educational opportunities for our sisters who could attend their colleges. Diversified work opportunities were expanded through the exchange of sisters from our community to others in the congregation.

In 1962, Pope John XXIII shook the hierarchy and many of the laity of the church with the introduction of the Second Vatican Council. The documents resulting from Vatican II would have a profound impact on the lives of all sisters and members of the church. Fresh air was sweeping through the centuries of stodgy old church customs, including the archaic rules of religious communities. Latin was discontinued as the ceremonial language of the church. The Latin Divine Office, the prayer of religious communities and priests, was replaced with the vernacular English. We finally understood what we were reciting during the multiple times of day we recited the verses of scripture.

One of the documents of Vatican II, *Perfectae Caritatis*, specifically called for nuns to reexamine the work of their founders, serving the poor, the sick, and the uneducated. The directive given was to "open the doors" of the convents to the people. We were given a mandate to reach out to those we served.

Many of the centuries-old convent traditions were set aside. The rigorous practices limiting individual freedom to think and to make decisions slowly altered. Demeaning penitential customs, practiced in the name of holiness, were discontinued in favor of sensible adult decision-making. It no longer made sense for adult women to kneel and ask for a penance for accidentally breaking a dish. Actually, it never made sense, but we did it in the name of obedience. Our convent doors opened, accepting families into the sisters' dining room to have meals with us, rather than relegating them to a separate room away from the cloistered part of the building. Too late for me, but I would have appreciated the new freedom to travel home when my father died.

The doctrines encouraged lay participation in ownership of the church. The Vatican II Council declared the church to be "the people of God." The people of the church were no longer seen as just belonging to the church, they *were* the church. They were part of the governing body. The nuns continued building on their freedom.

Religious communities were encouraged to build team-governing styles. With consensus-style governing, individuals were allowed participation in decisions in lieu of accepting blind obedience.

Changes were happening fast. Chapter meeting agendas were filled with controversial topics requiring discussions and votes. The Congregation asked that the incendiary topic of modification of the habit be put on our agenda. The degree to which changes were accepted as the norm in communities was largely dependent on the superior in charge. Superiors had to temper the introduction of changes so as not to alienate older sisters who had lived their entire adult lives by these ancient customs of silence, seclusion, child-like obedience, and medieval garb. For some, adherence to those rules was their measure of holiness. It was their security. To disrupt their pattern of living was tantamount to sacrilege. It shook the very foundation of their religious lives. They were not used to making their own decisions.

At the same time, many of the younger generations, more in tune with the social changes of the world, were eager for change. The generation in between—respected by the older and the younger—deserved credit for melding old customs with new policies. Their ready openness to change helped older sisters understand and gradually tolerate the turmoil, even though they might not fully accept it. Tensions could run high during decision-making chapter meetings.

Like many, I was reluctant at first and slow to come on board with innovations. I found myself confused about tearing away the vestiges of what my religious life had been thus far. After getting accustomed to the archaic rules and sometimes painful practices, I accepted them and no longer judged them. So, at first, I was not one to question the rules of the centuries. I felt those customs symbolized the holy life of a nun that I was striving to achieve. The external signs of holiness—bowed head, eyes down—were relatively easy for me to put on. It took considerable soul searching over the years to understand the difference between acting prayerful and being spiritual. I look back and wonder if I ever really made the distinction while in the convent. My understanding of the changes came slowly; I felt wearing the habit and veil was a safeguard against temptations. Finally, I came to accept that stripping away the camouflage was not the same as stripping away the holiness. I had yet to achieve a spirituality that had nothing to do with what I wore.

In retrospect, I know I didn't understand the impact Vatican II was having on the church as a whole and on our convent in particular. Change always comes with struggle. My life was good and I didn't particularly want to disrupt it. I was in my early thirties and just feeling secure in my vocation and my place in the community—teaching at the Academy.

Insulated as we were, I didn't grasp the dynamics of what was happening across the American Church and in religious communities throughout the country. Nor did I realize that our religious community was a mere speck in the overall picture of social changes happening at large. I could only see the effects in my own small world. The bigger picture would come with time and finally I would wake up to the importance of Vatican II in our lives.

Chapter Eighteen – *Exploring Changes*

$$\equiv$$

*T*he opportunity to experience effects of change came when Sister Joann called me into her office.

"How would you like to be a chaperone on the student trip to Europe with me this summer?"

"Are you serious?" I knew she and Sister Stephen were scheduled to chaperone the trip.

"Sister Stephen has been granted a study program at Sophia University in Tokyo this summer. She opted for it rather than the European trip."

It was an eight-week tour—spending two weeks each in England, France, Italy, and Switzerland. Students received credit for a government study program. While they attended classes each morning, the chaperones were free to sightsee. The only catch—I had to come up with eight hundred dollars for the trip. Not bad for eight weeks in Europe, but I had only one possible source. I presented my case to my mother who helped me out. She was thrilled to give me the opportunity.

"This will be your next graduation present," she said, reserving the right to exact something in return.

"How short do you want it?" Sister Camilla asked as she measured me for a modified habit for the trip, a concession granted by the superior. Sister Camilla—my former geometry teacher—managed a team of sisters who made all community habits. As head seamstress, she was in the sewing room nearly every minute she was not in the classroom. Sister Joann and I were among the first to wear a short dress—even before it was voted on by the community.

Here I go, I thought, *designing my own outfit; the genie is out of the bottle.* The dress was cut just below the knee, sleeves were three-quarter length with a white cuff, a simple, straight fabric hung in front and back simulating the scapular of our habits. A white, Peter Pan collar softened the neckline. The long veil, stiff headband, and white pleated coif were abandoned in favor of a short black veil edged in white and fastened behind the head, set back far enough in front to expose bangs.

We had our passport pictures taken in the new dresses. Sister Joann and I decided this outfit would be our official dress, but we felt a need for street clothes to be more comfortable and inconspicuous while traveling the streets of Europe. On a trip to our homes before leaving, we took the opportunity to raid the closets of our sisters-in-law for dignified but easy, traveling clothes. Mother took me to buy a pair of comfortable walking shoes. Our black tie, oxford heels looked much too awkward with the short-skirted dress and definitely out of place with dress clothes.

I went shoe shopping again in Decatur dressed in full habit this time. Fussy about style, I asked the puzzled sales person, "Are you sure this square, low heel pump will stay in style for a while?" The scene was a complete reversal of when I tried on the black, oxford heels of a nun with capri pants as a teenager. My mother, always a good sport, went right along with the incongruity, acting like it was perfectly normal for nuns to want stylish shoes.

The Academy girls freaked out a bit when we appeared in our short dresses, but they really freaked out when we came out in street dress and no veil the second day on the trip. It was a good experiment for me. I found it much easier to relate to the other chaperones. It worked both ways. We were the only Catholic nuns on the trip.

The charter flight across the water consisted of a hundred and twenty students from all over the country—boys and girls from both public and Catholic schools. It was like flying in a winged can of sardines vibrating with chatter and music. Takeoff and landing were the only times the aisles were clear. We first landed in England, staying at the University of Nottingham—Robin Hood territory. Tours took us to London to see the changing of the guard at Buckingham Palace, and other sites. We picnicked at Stratford-on-Avon.

Farm girl that I am, I asked the university personnel if I could possibly visit a typical English farm. A local Rotary Club member picked me up and drove me to his university research model farm. His wife served us tea in their quaint kitchen with Laura Ashley type decor. Zipping over the narrow countryside roads in his compact car on the 'wrong' side of the road was a bit frightening. He took me as his guest to a Rotary meeting luncheon. It was rare for them to have a woman as a guest; little did they know they had a nun.

"Tell us about yourself and what brings you to England." They questioned me on the student tour and how different farm life was in my youth. I responded to every question, leaving out only the part about being a nun.

We stayed in the village of Bordeaux in France. The Academy girls loved the smallness of Bordeaux. They could go to the village and hang out with new friends they made and mingle with the locals. Versailles and Paris were the major excursions away from the local campus. Finding a bathroom around the streets of Paris became an urgent challenge. The little French I had studied was helpful, but "WC" did not translate well. By the time we discovered one, the primitive conditions didn't matter. The customary "hole in the ground" was better than nothing.

Large and small planes, buses, and trains carried our group from country to country. We encountered cows eye-to-eye as the smallest plane rumbled to a stop in a French farmer's pasture. It must have been a common occurrence because the cows weren't startled. We felt it was tantamount to an emergency landing as there had been a question of total weight before we took off.

Geneva, Switzerland offered the finest accommodations in a first class hotel, a setting out of a Cary Grant movie. A stone walk led to a dining courtyard laden with white cloth covered tables. Fashionably dressed guests dined overlooking sunken gardens with stone steps leading to landscaped floral scenes. Local city officials treated the students royally, resulting in the study of Swiss government as their favorite course.

An elderly, elegant French woman grabbed my hand as we passed. "God bless you, we will be forever grateful to you Americans," she said. Our history students understood that she was expressing her feelings for the Allied liberation of France during World War II. Unfortunately, many of the younger French generation lacked the same gratitude.

During our two weeks in Rome, young Romeos hanging around our hotel became a familiar sight. Though cautioned, the girls enjoyed the whistles as they peered out the hotel windows. They didn't seem to mind the pinches experienced at every venture outside the hotel either. The pinchers didn't discriminate by age; we were all subject to their attention. I wondered if they would have pinched Sister Joann and me if they knew we were nuns. A side trip to Venice, including a gondola ride, a visit to Notre Dame Cathedral, and evening gatherings at St. Mark's Square captured the romantic ambience of Italy. I became deathly ill in Firenze. I saw only the inside of a hotel bathroom and missed all the art and famous statuary.

Monte Cassino, the monastery where St. Benedict founded his order of monks, was near the city of Rome. Sister Joann and I doubted we would ever be so near to the Monastery again, so we felt we had to attempt a visit to the origin of our Benedictine life. On a day the students were in classes, we ventured out on our own with a Eurail Pass to reach the site of our Benedictine heritage. We found a cabdriver in the village at the foot of the mountain who understood our attempts at sign language and our exaggerated pronunciation of *Mon-te Cas-si-no Mon-as-tery* as we pointed toward the monastery at the peak of the mountain. From the village, the monastery appeared to be a spec at the top. We prayed he understood that we needed a round-trip ride. After negotiating that excursion and successfully returning back to the hotel, I felt I could get anywhere I wanted.

Only a few days before leaving Rome and heading back to the United States, Sister Joann and I returned to our room after lunch to an alarming discovery.

"Joann, I th—think I've been robbed!" I stuttered.

"What do you mean?"

"My suitcase has been ripped open and messed up. The inside lining is torn away."

"What are you missing?"

"I don't think I am missing anything. My camera and purchases made in Versailles are still there."

I could find nothing missing; it was peculiar. We reported it to the tour manager only to find that another chaperone had the same experience.

The hotel authorities asked if I had any drugs with me that someone might have been searching for.

"Of course not," I explained, not at all sure he believed me. It was a moment when wearing the habit might have lent credence to my response.

Jack, the other chaperone, explained a cameo was missing. "I purchased it in Firenze for my mother."

We sat on a bench at the police department in Rome. Passing policemen looked at us suspiciously. I felt more the criminal than the victim. In Italy, you are guilty until proven innocent.

"My suitcase wasn't even locked, was yours? They tore up the latch trying to get into it."

Jack replied, "Mine wasn't either. It was like they were searching for something specific. They left other valuables. I don't think the cameo was their main objective."

The tour manager tried valiantly, if in vain, to interpret for the authorities who concluded we were a couple in the same hotel room. The whole episode was bizarre. I must admit, Jack was handsome in a rugged way—a dark-haired, pipe-smoking history teacher in tweeds— and my mind swirled with the fantasy of intrigue and romance in Rome. A Hollywood screenplay could have been written based on our singular shared experience. I dashed the fantasy from my thoughts. I was a nun after all, and touring with a group of high school students wasn't exactly a script for a Grace Kelly *Roman Holiday* movie.

Officially, police concluded a drug smuggler at the Swiss hotel had hidden drugs in the lining of our suitcases and then retrieved them in Rome. A feasible scenario because a man had joined our tour in Geneva and traveled with us to Rome—supposedly affiliated with the hotel. It may have been a clandestine way to get the drugs into the country without detection. Our luggage was never searched as we crossed borders. Perhaps that was a good thing; otherwise, they might have found drugs on both of us. It gave us the creeps to think someone had been keeping an eye on us, just waiting for the opportune time to get into our rooms. But, why would he choose two different rooms? There must have been more to the story than we ever knew.

Venice was the last side trip before leaving Rome. I bought a blue-black-tan striped canvas piece of luggage at a shop in St. Mark's

Square. The style was uniquely Venetian, and distinctly different from my conservative, gray Skyway piece.

We arrived back in New York weary from travel. After European collegiate accommodations for weeks, the students literally got down on their knees and kissed the good ole U.S.A. *terra firma*. A customs officer detained me as we made our way through the customs line. The others went through with no problem. The officer looked at my passport, then at me, back at my passport, back at me. He didn't question me, but his serious demeanor made me nervous.

Finally, he grinned. "I hardly recognized ya, Sister. Welcome home," he said. The black veil and dress on my passport picture didn't quite match my short-cropped hair and the polka dot outfit I wore on my return.

Chapter Nineteen – *A Change of Habits*

════

As a result of Vatican II, nearly all chapter meetings resulted in decisions and votes to part with some long-standing tradition. Modification of the habit was a major change.

Eight weeks in comfortable street clothes and no veil had swayed my position on modifying the habit. Without hesitation, I cast my vote in favor of a change. The medieval garb worn for centuries was voted out. The long habit was transformed to a more comfortable style—a street length skirt and abbreviated veil with no pleated coif around the neck and no stiff band on the forehead. In deference to the older sisters, the clothing change was optional. For some, it took years to make that transition, but all sisters in our community did make the change. Once the initial break with the traditional habit was made, it didn't take long before we transitioned into regular civilian clothes. Veils were eliminated. Some preferred to wear the habit in their outside work, while changing to street clothing inside the convent, much as anyone would change from work clothes to casual clothes after work.

In the history of women's fashion, all women, including nuns, wore long dresses until after World War I. Religious women wore conservative styles of the day, usually in gray or black. After the war, the trend toward shorter, above-the-ankle lengths became popular. Nuns, however, continued to wear the long dresses preferring not to expose their ankles. Not until the late sixties did they get back in step, dressing conservatively, but with the customs of the times.

The vote to go from a modified short habit to wearing secular dress was a brief stumbling block for me because I knew my penchant for style. I felt my desire for coordinating outfits would run amuck if we discarded the safety of uniformity. My initial intention was to vote against the step to allowing street clothes, but after the European experiment, I caved and voted for it. My vanity of dress would have to stay in check. My religious life may have started with the romantic notion of wearing veils and long flowing robes, but dressing in the style of the times made more sense.

With the resurrection of my 4-H sewing skills and creative fashion sense, I went to work on a new wardrobe. Individual allowances for clothing were very small; it took all my creativity to materialize a few outfits. I borrowed one of Sister Sheila's Home Economics department sewing machines and kept it buzzing in the back room of the St. Joe Hall dormitory at first with black suits with white collar and cuffs and then on to coordinating colors. I knew it would happen. My pent-up creative juices began to flow again.

Joanie, one of my typing students, spent her summers working in a clothing factory in her hometown. She offered to bring me and Sister Sheila a couple of conservative dresses from the factory. Thanks to Joanie, the bargain price of $3 helped us stretch our meager monthly allowance of $35, which had to cover all clothes and personal needs. The allowance came about with other decisions voted on in chapter meetings. Rules were relaxed. We were given the privilege of becoming responsible adults rather than dependent children. Money management was not part of the training that came with the allowance, probably because there was so little to manage.

All major decision-making meetings were held in August when all the sisters arrived home from summer school. We spent hours in the school auditorium in the comfortable blue upholstered seats discussing the pros and cons of changes. Raw emotions erupted over minor issues. Change is difficult, especially when centuries of customs are discarded with such momentum. There was a movement to let sisters return to their given names. The chapter voted in favor of it for those who wished to do so. Many sisters changed—particularly those with masculine names. With that new directive, though I didn't have a masculine name, I was happy to take back the name given to me by my mother. She loved it too. Sister Mary Ann became my third name since entering—from "Miss" Mary Ann (using no family name), to Sister Mary Magdalen, to Sister Mary Ann Cahill.

The relaxation of rules and a fast track to secular clothes and names resulted in some sisters resuming personal habits they found hard to discard at the time of entering. Smoking and drinking surfaced with the new independent freedom. Benedict had something to say about drinking. Rule, Chapter 40 stated: *Those to whom God gives the strength to abstain must know that they will earn their own reward.* On the other hand, regarding the sick, the Rule states: *With due regard for the infirmities of the sick ...a half bottle of wine a day is sufficient for each.* (Rule, Ch. 40) A generous amount, easily abused. Perhaps not so in Italy, but in current times in convents and monasteries, if you were prone to drinking, a half bottle of wine would be tempting enough to *drive* a person to their sick bed. I don't remember that the directive of the Rule was ever practiced.

As far as I can remember habits of drinking and smoking were never voted on in chapter, but sisters began to smoke and have a cocktail occasionally—usually in private rooms or small groups. Sometimes the groups became a bit like cliques. If you didn't smoke or drink with them, you could feel left out. Smoking was one thing, but cliques were another, incompatible with Benedict's rule where he quotes scripture. *They should each try to be the first to show respect to the other.* (Romans 12:10) The parish priest invited sisters to his home for an after-dinner cocktail and good conversation of an evening. It was open to all, but few participated.

I never had a smoking habit before I entered so it didn't make sense to take it up just because we could. I admit to enjoying the pleasure of a glass of wine or a social scotch and water occasionally. The hazards to health from smoking eventually caused many to let go of that practice for good. The novelty of drinking also subsided. Both were expensive habits, unnecessary bites in the small allowances we received.

Mother Clarisse was the Prioress of the community through most of the transition years. She worried about the welfare of the sisters as the restrictions, rules, and traditions relaxed. Of major concern was the fear that the new-found freedom might stimulate an exodus of sisters from the community. Mother Clarisse was an unassuming, soft-spoken superior who kept her sense of humor through it all.

"Oh, for the days when they were simply overjoyed with a Pepsi at recreation," she confided to one of the former sisters visiting her.

Difficult as it was to gracefully guide us through those years, Mother Clarisse was the perfect person to do it. Her understanding and acceptance of Vatican II documents was visionary. She was the first superior to accept the course that some of the sisters chose in seeking works beyond teaching; she initiated social work endeavors. Under her leadership, sisters were sent to poor southern Alabama parishes to work with children deprived of schooling and simple social activities; they began missionary work in Mexico and Chile. For the first time sisters staffed Newman Centers, clubs for Catholic students on secular university campuses.

Mother Clarisse sanctioned the leadership Sister Stephen took during the Civil Rights era in the 1960s by initiating and organizing a freedom march. Sisters and students proudly marched through the streets of Nauvoo singing, "We shall overcome . . ." while the citizens of tiny Nauvoo abandoned the streets, fearful of even watching, lest a riot break out. It wasn't the same as marching through Birmingham, but we knew we were standing up to be counted. We were overcoming our own tardiness in supporting the social justice.

Sisters at the convent became more involved with the local civic community. In the fearful days of the atomic bombs destroying life as we knew it, local Nauvoo leaders planned a training day to instruct citizens on what to do in the event of such a disaster. A civic building was prepared for the twenty-four-hour "bomb shelter" for survival training. The event was open to all local citizens. A few sisters from the monastery stepped up to do their civic duty by participating. The "shelter" was equipped with food, water, makeshift toilet facilities, Geiger counters, disaster training manuals, and little else. There were about two dozen men and women. Instructions on lifesaving techniques and emergency training were given. Survival emergency treatments were practiced on "radiation victims." One man designated as a victim was "stricken." While the group evaluated how to save him, seriously sober Sister Camilla came to his rescue.

"Maybe we should try mouth-to-mouth resuscitation," she volunteered.

As she bent down to administer mouth-to-mouth, the "victim" miraculously recovered without her assistance.

Historically, as a community we were blessed with the right leadership at the right time. The presence of the Holy Spirit was with the community at every election in the succession of superiors despite attempted human intervention. Not only had local priests influenced some elections in the past, but in-house politics played a role as well. In my time, Sister Rose was known to influence votes among the elderly sisters. She was not one to seek an elected position, but it was not beyond her to influence election outcomes. When sick sisters were confined to their rooms on the infirmary floor and unable to come down to the chapter meeting to vote, she would pay them a visit.

"Did you vote the right way, Sister?" she was heard to say as she picked up their votes. They would of course follow her "wise" advice.

One sister told me how, when she was first allowed to vote, Sister Rose approached her saying, "You do know how to place your vote, don't you, Sister?" My friend got the distinct feeling she had just experienced a campaign nudge on *who* to vote *for*, not merely *how* to vote. As a young sister, my friend was shocked at the blatant politics in a convent election.

In 1925, Mother Mercedes, the only superior to be elected for three terms, took the helm at a time when the community needed to be healed. In the early 1900s, a financial disaster plunged them into bankruptcy and great debt. They were in danger of losing everything and feared they would have to pack up and leave Nauvoo. Father Leonard Tholen was assigned by the Bishop as the local parish administrator and as financial adviser to the sisters. He is credited with saving the community from financial disaster. Not until 1921, did the community become solvent again. Mother Mercedes, sometimes called "the iron woman," spent much of her three administrations economizing, saving, reducing the debt, and restoring the community's credit. I didn't realize it at the time, but I later saw that as an Academy student out begging with Sister Innocents, I had a miniscule part in maintaining the community solvency.

Mother Ricarda, who took office in the forties, was a refined intellectual, almost mystically religious. She responded to Pope Pius XII's directive for convent women to seek higher education by implementing and accelerating the community's education program. Perhaps one of her biggest accomplishments was bringing the community under Pontifical rule, rather than under the control of the Diocesan Bishop. Sisters seeking dispensations from vows over the years were at the mercy of the sitting bishop's approval. Since bishops needed sisters to staff diocesan schools, they were reluctant to allow a single desertion. Under Pontifical rule, the community was allowed to accept ministries outside the diocese for the first time.

Mother Mary Paul, the superior elected following Mother Ricarda's term, inspired the young women of the novitiate during her time as directress of novices. I entered just after she was elected superior and never experienced her as my novice mistress. Known for a charisma that drew many to religious life, she inspired a fierce loyalty among her novices. The novitiate numbers grew under her direction. Her deep, dark eyes looked into souls and warned of the dangers to their vocations of devil temptations. I was in awe of her, but never felt her charisma.

Some in Mother Mary Paul's novitiate spoke of how she preached "giving up on their vocations would be giving in to the devil." Abandoning their vocations was not an option she would consider. Young women, drawn to her leadership, and loyal to her teaching, stayed longer than they might if they had followed their own conscience. The role of novice mistress held power. Some who grew up under her guidance spoke of her charm and sense of humor. She inspired them to be holy women, to develop independent thinking, and to make noble sacrifices. Several under her formation became leaders in the community, though several of those leaders later left.

Mother Clarisse was elected Prioress to follow Mother Mary Paul, who died of a brain tumor at age fifty-four. Mother Clarisse had been the acting principal at the Academy during my senior year. She replaced Sister Rose who took a leave of absence for her health.

Sister Rose held an unauthorized authority in the community illustrated more than once by her influence at elections of a Prioress. Over the years, I heard stories of her influence, but none more direct than one in the early sixties.

After completing Mother Mary Paul's term and just prior to the next election, Mother Clarisse was planning to clean out her desk and not accept another term.

Knowing this, the powerful Sister Rose, attempted to urge Sister Joan Cook, chemistry teacher at the Academy, to accept the election of Prioress.

"You've got to be the next Prioress," she told the young sister. Only in her thirties, Sister Joan Cook was stunned by the suggestion; a sleepless night followed. She had the distinct feeling Sister Rose was saying "I can make it happen." It was a frightening prospect to one so young who had never entertained such an idea or would she ever.

Never one to seek privilege or status, Mother Clarisse had already determined not to accept the Prioress position if elected. However, she sought counsel from a priest as to accepting God's will if elected. She was elected and served as Prioress for two terms—twelve years. Sister Rose never spoke of her suggestion to Sister Joan Cook.

Mother Clarisse, a small, soft spoken woman, a historian who championed social justice causes, led the community in implementing the changes dictated by the Council of Vatican II. It was no small task to stand before the community in meeting after meeting leading polarizing opinions to a consensus. The momentum of change in society and in the community resulted in 17% of the professed sisters leaving the community between 1960 and 1970. Not included in that percentage are the sisters in temporary vows who left. One by one, Mother Clarisse accepted requests from sisters wanting dispensations from their vows. Her fragile frame, yet strong shoulders carried the sisters through the crisis of diminishing numbers.

Chapter Twenty – *A Changing Academy*

===

*A*new assignment for Academy principal resulted as Sister Joann's
term ended. Sister Joan Cook, who had Academy experience
as a student and later as a Chemistry teacher, took over as the new
principal. Following the directives of the Council of Vatican II, she
envisioned a different kind of administration—a team leadership.
Under her creative vision, a dual administration was formed. She
led the academic and overall management as Principal, while Sister
Mary Pat, Dean of Girls, handled residential concerns. Following
Sister Mary Pat, I stepped up as Dean of Girls. I continued teaching
business classes as well. No longer a prefect, I kept long office hours
in the dorm seven days a week.

By the late sixties, enrollment at the Academy was showing a
gradual decline. Fewer families were sending their daughters to a
boarding school for a wholesome Catholic education. Fewer girls
considered boarding school an adventure as I once did. Though the
Academy facilities were new and the curriculum comprehensive,
public schools appealed to teenagers with the vast number of extra-
curricular opportunities they offered.

Parents were sending their daughters away to school for reasons
commonly associated with the few boarding schools today—structure

and discipline. Many parents sought out the school because of a broken home, or to remove their daughter from negative influences in relationships. Parents sought guidance and academic discipline for their daughters. Since the sisters devoted all their time to the welfare of the girls in their care, the small campus allowed little opportunity to stray.

I joined a nucleus of faculty members who grew concerned about the changing enrollment and the future of the school. We studied statistics and brainstormed options to stave off the decline in enrollment—once at a high of 253 students in 1964. Enrollment was declining and changing. No longer were the small-town country girls seeking the boarding school life. The closing of several grade schools in the Peoria Diocese once staffed by our sisters, contributed to the decline in Academy enrollment. Without the presence of sisters teaching in the parish grade schools, there was no encouragement for eighth graders to enroll at the Academy. Over time, young girls attending hometown, consolidated public schools had no awareness of the sisters' influence. Fewer "Hail Mary" girls attending the Academy resulted in fewer girls entering religious life. Without the steady number of girls becoming nuns, the community gradually decreased; staffing small town Catholic schools was no longer possible. Changes brought about by Vatican II were reverberating in convents across the country.

The changing student population increasingly required more counseling, more discipline, and more security. The Academy no longer functioned simply as an exemplary educational institution; it needed to be a social work service as well. Being good listeners and armchair counselors did not equip the sisters to deal with the severe family situations encountered, as well as new disciplinary problems.

Long discussions among the concerned nucleus of sisters resulted in a written proposal for a formal study regarding the future of the school. Those of us who signed the proposal wanted the community to know our concerns. We loved the school; it was *alma mater* for many of us. We didn't want it to decline in enrollment or reputation, but we felt it was not feasible to continue if everything was status quo. We could not ignore the changes of the past twenty years. On the outside looking in, it might have looked the same, but increasing discipline problems, attention seeking suicide threats, and heartbreaking personal stories from students painted a different picture for those of us close to the situation. I sat across the desk from parents desperate for help; sometimes single parents who needed our support. Those were not rare cases, they were common.

The drafted proposal expressed not only concerns, but options to consider for the future. It emphasized the need for more counseling personnel as their roles changed from addressing college applications and majors to assisting with more dire life problems. The school needed counselors who could deal with extremes situations. We felt the mission of the school should be directed toward "at risk" students. Such a shift would dramatically alter the original purpose of instructing young ladies in the arts and sciences; it would require specialized personnel.

Though there were several sisters in on the discussions from time to time, when it came time to sign our names on the final proposal, only nine brave souls signed it. Sister Joan Cook offered it to Mother Clarisse to take before the council with the recommendation that the community discuss it at a chapter meeting.

My life changed on the day that proposal was presented to the chapter meeting with the professed sisters in attendance. The number of sisters was smaller than usual since not all sisters from missions were home during the spring chapter meeting. We anticipated a discussion, not a vote, so the smaller numbers did not concern us. I could not have anticipated or imagined the outcome of the meeting.

We, of course, anticipated some opposition to our ideas, but we hoped that our presentation would lead to a healthy discussion.

Chapter meeting agendas include the business of the community, everything from major building acquisitions to the length of a veil. Long discussions ensued on nearly every topic. The response to our researched proposal was beyond the realm of anything I could have foreseen.

We thought the proposal was meritorious. We assumed no premature decision; we wanted an informative discussion of ideas. We felt it important that all the sisters be aware of what we saw happening to the Academy's future. The mere suggestion of change in those times evoked controversy and anxiety, so we had deliberately avoided a threatening tone. Or so we thought.

The result felt like a bit of an ambush. It was obvious that a hostile, prepared response awaited us.

The main critique and official response came from one domineering presence—my nemesis from the day I enrolled at the academy as a freshman.

Sister Rose took the floor. We should have anticipated that she would return from her self-imposed exile for her health to make her case for the Academy's future. Often ill, she recuperated at her sister's home about thirty miles from the monastery. She was no longer a daily presence in the community, but was always in touch—especially when matters relating to the Academy were to be considered.

I shuddered at the sight of her figure laboriously rising from her chair, making her way to the front of the assembly, bypassing the speaker's podium. Her stage was the entire front of the large, terrazzo-floored, community room with its straight chairs arranged around long tables.

Sister Joan Cook and I looked at each other, mentally agreeing *Of course she would be there. Why hadn't we thought of that?* After all, she was by many, considered the authority on all things related to the Academy—past, present, and future. Presumably, her forty-one years as principal and directress gave her that authority. She had a mammoth interest in the continuing success of the school. It was her legacy, her heart. She risked the health of her heart that day— returning to defend her legacy.

I cringed at the familiar imposing black form still in full habit, hands tucked under the leather belt, heavily pacing the front of the room—her round, spectacled face flushed with determination. Her presence transported me back to high school morning assemblies, where I stood among her subjects anxiously awaiting her declarations.

With oratorical stature, she expounded on our proposal. Word by exclamatory word, paragraph by paragraph, the proposal began to look more pitiful with every syllable. She was presenting it as a document with one purpose—to destroy the reputation of previous decades of the educational institution. Peering through those thick spectacles, she never made eye contact. Her gaze stretched across the room above the heads and into the space beyond, as though she might be receiving a divine revelation or a directive straight from God. Her presiding presence struck a fear throughout the entire assembly and left them silenced and incapable of response.

Her counter to our proposal went something like this: "St. Mary's Academy is the foundation of this community. It is the reason our founding Sisters came to Nauvoo. To even consider abandoning the mission of educating young women from good Catholic families would undermine the dedication of the many sisters gone before us, who struggled to keep the doors open during years of financial crisis. And what would the dear girls of St. Mary's, who treasure their SMA diploma, think if their *alma mater* became a house known for girls with disciplinary problems?"

I knew we were doomed. It was as though she could not believe or even consider that present day students differed from the ones she wrote about in her book, *Letters to Ann*, published in 1963. Sister Rose's summation painted us as renegades who had dared to attack everything the community had sacrificed to preserve. Sister Joan,

Sister Sheila, and I looked at each other helplessly. We felt branded as the "naughty nine," ungrateful and disloyal to our hundred-year history, lacking in respect for the hundreds of girls who had graduated wearing the blue and white banner of loyalty.

Sister Rose continued to make her case as she paced the floor. "This community has struggled in years past to preserve the sterling quality of education for our dear girls of St. Mary's. As a community, we should preserve that tradition. A movement to change the makeup of the student body from wholesome young women to girls with problems would belittle the tradition of St. Mary's. Such a movement shows little loyalty on the part of those who propose it." Her speech may have lasted twenty minutes, but it seemed like hours.

Once she had spoken, no one dared offer a rebuttal. Hers was the final word. Such a singular attack was a colossal disappointment. There was no consideration of the merits of the plan or solutions offered to improve enrollment. No acknowledgment of the number of talented faculty members who had left the community, leaving fewer teachers to carry heavier burdens. Professional lay help would ultimately be required, a cost yet to be considered. No mention of the statistics that substantiated our proposal. No discussion at all.

The nine of us were devastated by the tirade, particularly Sister Joan and I, both graduates of the school. We had poured our heart and soul into the Academy. We'd loved the school from our days as students. I felt my posture slumping as Sister Rose paced the floor, never looking directly at us. Surely, my heart was cracking and bleeding inside my chest.

Sister Rose had spoken. It was definitive. The proposal died simply with her stamp of disapproval. We had hoped for more from our community of sisters, but they sat in silence. It was apparent no one believed the Academy to be in danger of closing, nor did they have any awareness, or understanding of the changing needs of the students.

Unprepared for the lack of response or support from members, I took it as a personal attack on my loyalty and dedication—not only to the school but to the community. I had given my life and my love to the Academy and to the community from the age of fourteen when I packed my blue and white Samsonite suitcase, left my family and home, and moved into second floor North Dorm. Early on, my dream had been to teach there and be a dorm prefect one day. I was doing exactly what I had always dreamed.

My thoughts ran rampant. How could they doubt my loyalty after years of living with them and giving years of service? I wondered if the sisters even knew the content of the proposal or if unfounded rumors preceded the chapter meeting. Other than hearing Sister Rose, I wondered how they would have known what had been proposed. There had been little introduction of the proposal. It was almost as if everyone knew of the proposal, but how could they? It had never been presented or circulated? We had given it to Mother Clarisse requesting it be put on the agenda for discussion at the next chapter meeting.

Fear would have been a normal reaction if the sisters thought our goal was to close the Academy. They would wonder about their future. Without the financial support of the Academy, what would happen to the community? What would happen to all of them? The Academy sustained the community. Fear can be gripping. It has the power to support irrational thought. Such thoughts become reactionary.

I searched the room for some sign of support from the group. Most eyes were down, veils shrouded others. I could truly understand a lack of courage to stand up to Sister Rose. Her powerful voice was too strong for anyone to dare contradict. I was no better. I had never been able to stand up to her; certainly not in that situation.

My normal strength gave way to a helpless glob of tears while she mercilessly criticized us and our ideas. I couldn't believe what I was hearing. She never named names, but I felt her trashing my credibility and character right before my eyes. I could not stay to hear her summation. Through my tears, it was all I could do to find my way along the windowed wall and out of the large recreation room. I almost ran down the terrazzo hallway and out the heavy front door of the convent. Sister Joan was too strong to collapse as I did. Sister Sheila shed silent tears.

For days, I asked myself how they could not know me after I had lived among them for so many years. How could they think that I would be part of a plan to destroy the place I loved? My gut suffered a blow never experienced before. Most of those who had signed the proposal seemed to continue unscathed.

The proposal was dismissed that day. I felt dismissed as well. Three days passed before I could participate in community events in the convent building. I took refuge in my room at the Villa House across the street from the school. Wallowing in rejection, I skipped prayers and formal meals for days. My heart was damaged.

The strange silence of the community remained an unsolved puzzle for me. However, the rule of silence served as a shield, allowing me to move among everyone with limited participation in daily activities. I took refuge in my work at the Academy.

I never saw Sister Rose again.

Chapter Twenty-One –
Experimental House

I finished the school term after the fateful chapter meeting, but I lost heart in working for the future of the school. I went through the motions of fulfilling my duties, but I never felt the same. Alternative plans for the school were never brought up again. I knew I needed a change.

Another proposal—this time unrelated to the Academy—was drawn up by Sister Joan Cook in response to the changes occurring in our community lives, in the Catholic Church, and in the world. Following the directives of Vatican II, Sister Joan proposed an experimental house of Nauvoo Benedictines. A house, or mission, made up of sisters in diverse works. Sisters who were attracted to new service endeavors joined the innovative mission. Several who lived in the experimental house went into the local community as nurses, social workers, and teachers.

The house was to be a prototype for living an open community life while staying true to our Benedictine Rule—a model for other missions to adopt. Many communities in other parts of the country were adopting similar small missions based on service to the people. Mother Clarisse accepted the proposal. I couldn't help but wonder if her approval was a consolation prize for letting the Academy proposal disintegrate.

Everyone who accepted the experimental mission house assignment agreed to the innovative structure. There was to be no superior in charge. After years of asking permission for every move they made, participants experienced freedom to make their own decisions and manage their own lives as any professional woman would. Together, we made community decisions.

Upon reflection, I am not really sure if I requested a transfer from the Academy or if it was felt that my presence was a detriment to its future. I finished the school year and obediently accepted my next assignment to Alleman High School, a co-ed Catholic school in Rock Island, Illinois, where I taught business subjects and commuted from the new experimental house.

Sisters Joan, Sean, Sandra, and I, all part of the "naughty nine," shared the mission house in Moline, Illinois, with a group of six other sisters who taught school or worked in other ministries in the Quad City area.

Sister Joan Cook became principal at the parish grade school in Moline. Sister Sean, who had been the convent and academy nurse, helped start the Neighborhood Health Center in Rock Island. After years of confinement to the infirmary floor of the convent, Sister Sean felt liberated in the new environment and for the first time "felt a part of the community."

The experimental mission house had a happy and relaxed atmosphere. We followed monastery rules—praying together in the little chapel at scheduled times, keeping the customary silence, and running a frugal household. All of us were involved in preparing the budget. Unlike any other mission school, where the parish pastor sent teacher stipends to the monastery, our paychecks came to our house. We learned to live off what we earned and sent the bulk of the money to the monastery.

Preparation of meals was rotated as Benedict directed. The sisters ... *should serve one another ... no one will be excused from kitchen service unless he is sick or engaged in some important business of the monastery, for such service increases reward and fosters love.* (Rule, Ch. 35)

The dining room adjoined the small kitchen on the basement level. Guests were invited to join us at meals, a practice never before allowed.

The recreation room, our evening hangout where we watched television—a recent perk—read, or corrected student papers, was a depressing room with dull, mismatched furniture. Typical small basement windows above eye level provided minimum light bouncing off the black-topped parking lot. A stark white wall and overhead fluorescent lighting did little for the ambience of the room.

Each evening at recreation, my creative juices salivated to make over the space in a way that would lift its slumping spirit before it affected ours.

"What would you think of redecorating this room?" I suggested to the group at recreation one evening.

"How do you mean?" A series of legitimate questions followed. "What kind of decorating could we do? Do we have the budget for it?"

"All this brown, gloomy furniture is depressing and not even functional. It needs some color and life. I think we could do it with minimal costs if we all help. I have some ideas."

We discussed it at a group meeting and reached a decision, a resounding commitment to the project. My vision was something modern looking—maybe red, white, and black. Sister Cecile and I spray painted the cinder block window wall black, leaving the other three walls white. We put red slipcovers from Target over the stuffed chairs. A cousin of Sister Sean's came over with his circular saw and cut a long, formica-topped refectory table down the center lengthwise. One half attached to the long, white wall as a buffet table. The cousin cut down the legs on the other half and attached it to another wall for extra seating. Three plain white canvases attached to the wall above the buffet. Red and black felt pens hung nearby for guests to sign the canvases—*Voila*, a novel guest book.

Sisters Margaret, Audrey, and Sandra sat on the floor at evening recreation gluing soda cans together to form a three-foot cube. Topped with a sheet of acrylic, it became a coffee table. A perfect duplicate of a craft idea I had seen somewhere, except the original plan used Budweiser cans. A few task lights were added in lieu of the florescent. What a transformation. The red and black scheme might have looked a little like a bordello, but it lifted everybody's spirits, and it released my inhibited creativeness.

We invited faculty and staff from Alleman High School for an Open House when the room was completed. No one commented, but the open bar at the buffet probably surprised most, if not all, of our guests. We were the new kind of nuns.

I missed the Academy, the girls, and the sisters, but I enjoyed the new relationships and students at Alleman High School. Alleman was a diocesan Catholic co-ed school administered by the Clerics of St. Viator, a community of priests and brothers headquartered in Arlington Heights, Illinois. I loved the students and the athletic activities of the school as well as the camaraderie of the faculty—mostly lay people with several Viatorian priests and a few nuns. Sister Sandra and I were the only Benedictines.

While living in Rock Island, my reluctance to return to Nauvoo for any reason grew steadily. Real or imagined, I never felt the same acceptance as I walked through the monastery halls. Thoughts of leaving the community began to filter into my mind for the first time.

The number of Sisters in convents across America began to dwindle in the sixties and continued to decline until the late seventies. Some statistics indicate that the number of Sisters in America who left their convents between 1964 and 1974 dropped from a high of 186,000 to 86,000. They were leaving the rules and restrictions of their convents, but not necessarily leaving the Church. Some were called to new ministries. A myopic view of the decline offered individual reasons, but the broader view had to include the culmination of decades of directives from the Vatican, all meant to quell the rising independence of congregations of women religious.

Academy enrollment declined, fulfilling the statistical projections upon which we had based our proposal. The number of girls who entered the convent from the Academy declined. Each time a sister gave up her vows and returned to secular life it was jarring for those of us who remained. We lost dear friends and amazingly talented women from our ranks. Community life was unsettled.

The swinging doors may have prompted some to face the realization that they never belonged in a convent. Some had been counseled to stay during early years of questioning their vocation, but buoyed by the numbers leaving, they eventually summoned up their courage to join them. They no longer felt the pressure of "failure to persevere" or feared the "influence of the devil." Individualism had been denied for centuries in favor of producing cookie-cutter nuns. The days of nuns being manipulated and moved at the will of the superior, even at the command of a parish priest or bishop, all in the name of obedience, were coming to a close.

Some sisters simply grew impatient with the community's slow response to diverse needs of the people. They felt they could work on behalf of the oppressed and the poor much faster as individuals on the outside. They could still do the work of the church while choosing their own ministries and making their own decisions.

We came to convent life to serve God by pledging obedience to the religious way of life. We came to give, not receive. We lived quiet lives in a camouflaged background. That changed with the directives of Vatican II in the document on religious life, Perfectae Caritatis. It became the catalyst for the changes.

The shift in attitudes, the new awareness of our own individual value, of our strengths and ability to make decisions based on our talents and ideas resulted in happier individuals in a common environment. As women religious, we were no different than women in all walks of life who were waking to their independence.

Though changes had evolved, it was still necessary to receive community approval to forge into a different ministry, whether mission work in Mexico, church work in Alabama, or counseling on college campuses.

I remember when Mother Clarisse announced the first Mexico mission. Sister Francine pioneered the first ministry outside the United States. Her work in an orphanage in Cuernavaca, Mexico, required that she study and become fluent in Spanish. She obtained special permission to wear a short habit and abbreviated veil. Everyone gathered in the dining room for the big reveal of the first modified habit. Mother Clarisse was wise to be open about it, rather than having Sister Francine slip out in secrecy for Mexico.

It was after lunch, our recreation time, so we could respond when we saw her. Sister Francine was one of the most beautiful of sisters. She had a small, slender frame, dark eyebrows, big dark eyes, and a beautiful smile. She was also one of the most brilliant and spiritual among us. It took bravery to walk the gauntlet of eyes not knowing how the sisters would react.

"She looks beautiful," one after the other commented.

"I like the look; it looks comfortable and still modest," they said.

"How does it feel without the headgear wrapped around your face?" someone asked.

"Feels great, but a little naked," Francine replied.

I thought the look was sensible and attractive while still un-mistakenly "nun" looking. It was months, maybe years, later before the community got around to the vote allowing everyone to wear a modified habit.

Though outreach ministries increased, there were still community commitments to parish schools. Superiors had to juggle the interests of individuals while still retaining commitments to parishes. As the number of sisters dedicated to teaching dwindled, pastors could no longer demand the same number to staff their schools.

At our Experimental House in Moline, more than ever before, I experienced life as a member of a civic community. Relating to students, parents, faculty, and friends beyond the confines of convent walls gave me a new perspective on living a religious life while serving the people of the Church. I was enjoying a new way of life. Our house structure allowed a more relaxed, but still prayerful existence. Sisters could come and go to their respective duties and events in the neighborhoods as needed. No longer were we mystery women in black garb, teaching by day and hidden by nightfall.

I enjoyed attending Alleman basketball and football games at night. Visibility at school events gave the people a sense that we were real people—like them in many ways. They could see us involved in local ministries. We were nurses, social workers, spiritual directors, as well as teachers.

Toward the end of the first year in the Moline house the idea of leaving the Nauvoo community kept creeping into my thinking. I never shared these thoughts with friends because I felt the idea had to be just a temporary temptation. After all, I had promised a vow of stability to this community. I wondered if the shakiness of my commitment resulted from the meeting in which Sister Rose questioned my loyalty.

I felt accepted and loved in the Moline house. Alleman was the perfect teaching assignment. I feared that future obedience assignments might not be so compatible. That uncertainty left me wondering if I could accept them. Never before had I felt that way.

Chapter Twenty-Two –
Decision to Leave

The summer chapter meeting was about to begin. Sister Sheila and I settled into the comfortable padded blue seats of the auditorium at the Academy. Spirits were buoyant. Most of the sisters were home from summer school for a few days before heading to new mission assignments. The next day I would be back in Moline, beginning another year at Alleman High. Sister Sheila was continuing in the Home Economics Department at the Academy.

We chatted about the contents of the large manila envelope full of papers pertaining to the agenda of the three-day meeting. There were new topics to be considered and ballots to vote for one thing or another. I became less and less tolerant of what seemed trite discussion topics. Should the modified habit be black or navy blue? How long or how short? Hours were spent haggling over such trivia while the future of the Academy and the convent were given little time on the agenda. The proposal of the "naughty nine" was never mentioned again. Sister Rose had effectively closed that case.

Even in the order of recitation of psalms, Benedict said . . . *we urge that if anyone...finds this unsatisfactory, he should arrange whatever he judges better . . .* (Rule, Chap. 18) What we deemed better for the Academy was not to be considered.

I looked around the auditorium at the dwindling membership— most of them were in their sixties and seventies. I was thirty-six. There were few younger. In my imaginary crystal ball, I could see myself closing the doors and turning out the lights of the convent when I was old and gray. Keeping the scary vision to myself, I shuddered at the scene.

My growing discontent with the lack of community progress toward making crucial decisions regarding the survival of the Academy and the convent, coupled with the uncertainty I felt about my acceptance in the community, led to more frequent thoughts of leaving. Was it just temptation or was I being directed to a new path? Whatever it was, I was listening. I hadn't yet put flesh to what I would do or how I would survive without the support to which I had been accustomed. That seemed premature. The thoughts were more like a fantasy of what if, rather than a reality. But then, thoughts create our reality. I had put a new reality in motion and the momentum was growing.

For three days, discussions continued. The best part for me was being with my good friends for those days. Meetings in the summer were always happy reunions. However, as the discussions droned on, my agitation increased. I became impatient with questions asked and answered over and over.

Mentally drained at the end of the last day, I turned to Sister Sheila. "I'll see you later, Sheila. I'm going to the dorm room Meet you at dinner."

I took my envelope with the packets of unfinished business and left the auditorium through the backstage where my path crossed Sister Audrey. She stopped me, apparently sensing something different in my demeanor.

"Are you all right?" she asked with her intuitive wisdom.

"I'm okay." After a brief exchange, I continued into the residence hall. I wasn't ready to talk about the way I was feeling. I sidestepped any attempt to discuss what was on my mind.

I passed my former office as I had done so many times before, crossed the large, teal carpeted foyer of Mary Hall, and climbed the familiar steps to the second floor of the dorm. The long, curved hallway was empty. I was walking with deliberation and purpose, as though on a mission—one born of frustration. Halfway down the hall, I stopped. I stood next to the incinerator chute in the wall. Almost robotically, I opened the heavy, metal door in an unintended yet deliberate way, looked into the dark cavity, took the manila envelope, and dropped it—with its entire contents—down the chute to the furnace.

That was the definitive moment, a symbolic gesture that signified the end. None of the material had meaning to me anymore. I didn't care about debating over one more vote. From that point forward, I began to face the future of a new life. The fantasy became reality.

Though I had not yet completely absorbed the symbolism of incinerating the past twenty years of my life in one stroke, it was not a frivolous act or an angry gesture. Something had died inside me. I knew the ramifications would be considerable. I had no plan. My mounting frustration had culminated in an instant decision. As with other major decisions in my life, I managed to face it and proceed with calculated planning and minimal day-to-day stress.

Making the transition from a life on the inside to life outside would call for facing the practicalities of the transition. With the decision came a certain peace, a feeling of freedom. Though there were unfamiliar mountains ahead of me, I felt I could climb them one step at a time, as long as I didn't panic. Fear causes anxiety, and anxiety can be paralyzing. I needed to move forward with confidence. I needed good thoughts to overcome fear of the unknown.

My mind swirled with questions to be answered. What would I do? Could I continue teaching at Alleman as a lay person? Did I want to? What would the students think? How does one get dispensation from lifetime vows of betrothal to Jesus?

I knew it was possible because others had done it before me. Still, it would be gut-wrenching. Twenty years of my life had gone into this commitment. I believed in it, but I was changing. The community was not, at least not in ways I anticipated, and not on my timetable. I didn't see the community growing. Members who had been here twenty, thirty, and more years were leaving. Young people who entered did not stay long. I had made a decision without a plan of survival. I knew I would have to stay calm and make calculated plans to move on with my life. Somehow, I knew I could do it. My soul's plan was changing, or, more likely, this *was* my soul's plan. I felt God's grace would be with me.

In retrospect, the 1970s were a tumultuous time in every religious community. It wasn't the ways of the world that were calling to sisters; it was more the work of the world. Sisters felt called to ministries other than teaching. Nuns weren't seeking a new identity; they were seeking the individual identities they had given up when they entered the convent. They wanted their creativity, their freedom to explore ideas, and, to a degree, their own personalities back.

Slow to the table, compared to others, it took the rejection on that famous proposal presentation day for me to realize that I wasn't valued and accepted in my own community the way I thought I was. The innovative ideas of our small group were not heard. I could no longer pursue fulfillment of the needs I saw in the changing clientele of the Academy. The girls who needed us were those on the verge of addictions, delinquency.

When the community rejected the ideas of the "naughty nine," I began to question the way we lived. How could we disregard the needs of the girls who lived within our reach? How could we stay secluded and secure within our convent walls and neglect the needs of society outside those walls? How could we equate conformity and anonymity with holiness and spirituality? Observance of the centuries-old rules and blind obedience did not contribute to piety, or if it did, it must have been a superficial piety.

Members who pioneered for change had proven the work of the church could be done without wearing identical, long, black, formidable outfits. No one had lost the respect that the habit supposedly garnered. If respect for nuns had been lost by the changing of their habits, then it had been shortsighted in the first place. On the contrary, we could witness for Jesus by reaching out to more people. We were no longer unapproachable. We were no longer the mysterious, untouchable creatures that slipped around two by two, eyes down, appendages hidden under a straight scapular and long skirt when we ventured into the public marketplace.

I remember talking with a parent of one of my second graders when I taught in Peoria, Illinois. We talked in the hall outside the classroom for a moment. During the quick conversation about his son, I laughed showing my big Irish smile.

"Wow," he said, "you should smile more often. You look friendlier." We laughed a lot behind convent walls, and I never thought of us looking sober or austere. Perhaps wearing black from head to toe could suggest that.

It was difficult to think of leaving my dearest friends. We had shared community life for so many years. I loved their quirks, their idiosyncrasies, and their humor. We knew every member in our small community.

Sister Sheila had given no indication of unrest in her vocation. I didn't want my doubts to cause her to waver in hers, so I didn't share my plans with her until near the end. We were close and yet I didn't seek her counsel. That may have been selfish and unfair. It may have been that I didn't want to defend my decision or be talked out of it.

As the school year progressed in Moline, I sensed that both Sister Joan and Sister Sean felt as I did. They had already made the determination to leave together though they hadn't yet requested a dispensation to finalize their decision. Their plans were to move out of state, to go west.

The hardest part of the planning stage for me was when and how to tell my mother about my decision. She had so proudly shared my accomplishments over the years with friends that I didn't want to disappoint her. She had such admirable strength after the death of my father. I hated the thought of adding disappointment or sadness to her life.

On a weekend trip home from Moline, I sat at the small kitchen table against the wall, eating my breakfast. Wearing her familiar floral-print, bibbed apron, she poured her coffee and sat down with me. We chatted about the progress of her beautiful roses in the backyard.

I blurted out, "Mom, I am thinking of leaving the convent. What would you think if I did?"

She was pensive for a moment, looked at me with that little sliver of an understanding smile on her lips, "I saw that coming."

"You did? How? When?"

"Remember some time back when you asked me if you could have a few of the extra glasses in my cupboard? The barrel glasses with *Chicago Bears* on them? Now what would you need glasses for, unless you weren't planning to use them in your own kitchen?"

"You are so observant and intuitive. You know me better than I know myself."

"I was just waiting for you to come to your decision before I asked. If it is what you want, Toots, it is what I want for you."

She had seen the signs over the past two years. There was no need to doubt her support. She had always been there for me.

I told my brother Joe the same weekend. He and David lived with my mother. They were both unmarried. David was disabled; Joe, the rock of the family.

At one time, Mother had all four boys at home. Irish families tend to marry late. In a way, I was just getting around to starting my life also.

Joe summed up what I imagined the other brothers would think. "I couldn't see why you joined in the first place," he said. "What are you going to do now?"

"I'll probably find a job teaching somewhere, though I'd like to find something in school administration. I've had enough of the classroom."

I asked Mother if she would tell Bill and Lois, Dick and Pat, and their families. My mother was always the filter through which family news came. I saw no need to call a family conference and make a dramatic announcement. I knew everyone would take it in stride. I had been away living the convent life for so long that they followed my path with interest but had no strong feelings about my direction. They understood that I was not leaving the Church, only the convent. If I had said I was leaving the Church, then I am sure I would have heard some opinions.

Approaching Mother Clarisse with my thoughts was the first *official* hurdle. Admitting to her I wanted to request a dispensation required almost more courage than I could muster. I feared the pain in her eyes. She was a gem of a woman, a woman of strength, camouflaged in Victorian delicateness. As acting principal in my last year of high school, she had made our senior year the best of the four. As a class, we never felt favored by Sister Rose; we had developed a bond with Sister Clarisse.

As Mother Clarisse, my superior, I still felt she was my champion, though I found it perplexing that she hadn't defended the merits of our proposal on the Academy's future. She had the tenacity to challenge Sister Rose, but she didn't. I never quite understood. She offered no explanation.

My memory is fuzzy as to when and where I approached Mother Clarisse with my decision and request, though the encounter was memorable.

"I'm afraid I have sad news today."

"What's wrong?" She spoke tenderly, patting her chest, her usual nervous gesture. I suspect she knew what was wrong, but didn't want to hear it.

In her gentle way, she accepted my decision with reluctance. Her heart was heavy, as was mine. Knowing it wouldn't help, she didn't contest my decision. She knew my spirit had been broken over the Academy proposal incident. She gave me a hug as we shed tears together. She would soon be ending her term in office. I was one of the last to request a dispensation under her authority.

We talked a few times before doing the paper work to petition a dispensation of my vows from the Holy See in Rome. Once the paper work was completed and signed, I needed to wait for the approval from Rome before I could leave. Though there was no guarantee it would be granted, I tried not to entertain that thought. I had no Plan B. A few months after I requested it, the final dispensation was granted on June 1, 1973.

Not all religious communities are tied so closely to Rome. Since we joined the Federation under Mother Ricarda's leadership in 1955, the Nauvoo Benedictines were part of a group of Benedictine convents. There was strength and power in numbers. As a member of the Federation of Benedictines, our community had petitioned and received permission to report to the Bishop of Rome, the Pope, rather than the bishop of the local diocese. No longer did community superiors have to obtain permission from the local bishops for decisions within the community. In the Federation, all dispensations had to be approved by Rome; they were granted with regularity in the 1960s and early 1970s.

I perhaps benefitted by the fact that many others had gone before me. Mother Clarisse's effort to change minds may have been weakened by the mid-70s. Our Nauvoo community of sisters was small. It was like a family. We asked permission of the superior before leaving the community. In some cases, the superior could and would make it difficult for a sister to leave or would not accept a request for a dispensation. There were situations where a sister—following her own conscience—sometimes felt forced to not return to the convent after her teaching year. In those cases, no dispensation was even requested. In effect, I suppose they were AWOL. That probably happened more often in bigger communities where members did not know each other as well as we did.

I said my goodbyes to Sister Joan and Sister Sean at the end of the school term in May 1973. Their meager belongings were packed and stacked into an old car. They headed west to Colorado, offering me an invitation to join them. It was painful to see them leave, but I needed to stay close to Illinois since my mother was aging. I also felt the need to be independent of living in community again, even a community of two or three.

My turn to pack was coming soon.

As I approached the end of a commitment to the vows taken years before, reflections on the day of my first vows came back to me.

I remembered my panic standing at the altar, discovering I had inadvertently omitted promising the vow of obedience. I remembered thinking my vows were not valid. I vowed stability and conversion of morals, but not obedience. Just as I thought then, maybe it was an omen.

Though we didn't specifically mention poverty, the promise of "conversion of morals" was a commitment to embrace all of monastic life, which included poverty and chastity.

I was able to take poverty in stride. Our family was not flush with material things when I was a child. Although looking back I cannot remember ever wanting for much, except a pair of popular huarache shoes. Mother thought I should always wear sensible shoes, not "a bunch of straps."

We came into the convent with little more than the clothes on our backs; everything was provided by the community. After the dress attire was relaxed, the allowance of $35 per month had to cover our clothes, toothpaste, and other toiletries.

We had to reinvent ourselves. Though poverty was an unquestioned way of life, we felt the pinch of stretching $35. Convent life provided a roof over our heads and meals on the table. Life was secure. Material possessions were not coveted.

Though I had some anxiety about facing life outside the security of the convent, the years of living with the restrictions of poverty served me well. Some religious orders give a stipend to help departing members get established. Many, maybe most, give little or nothing. Religious communities that require a dowry when entering, usually, but not always, return the dowry to the departing nun. The experiences of leaving a convent are as varied as the number of convents.

Sisters who leave before final vows are young. They usually go home for a transition period before seeking a job and living on their own. At thirty-seven I couldn't go back home even for an interim period. I needed to find a job and get on with my life. I could not expect to be supported as if still a teenager, nor did I want to go back to my hometown and face everyone's questions and stares.

I could imagine the dialogue, "Where's she been for twenty years?"

"I thought she was in a convent."

"Think she got kicked out?"

Most of my friends had already married and moved on anyway.

A loan from the community would have been helpful, but with so many leaving that could have been a hardship. A brief orientation to money management and a job search would also have been beneficial, but such a concept was never considered. After all, they weren't intentionally downsizing. Helping with the transition was never a part of the procedure when members left. No one in the community had the experience to provide training on how to search for a job and few could give money management advice. We made the choice to leave; it was up to us to figure out the survival steps. It was time to *shake the dust from our sandals* and move on.

Up to the point of leaving, I never needed a resume. Job security came with the annual assignment to teach. The pastor of the school where I was teaching sent the compensation to the Mother Superior. We never saw a check or even knew how much we were paid. Other than the $35 a month we began receiving, we never handled money. That amount hardly necessitated learning how to keep a checkbook. With the exception of mission superiors, who managed the household finances, women who left the convent were ill prepared for the financial experiences ahead. The true cost of living on their own was an unknown.

Consequently, many women fell into deeper poverty than they had known in community life. They encountered a stress not experienced before. Second-hand furniture and clothes are easy to live with, but a lack of income security and health benefits only added to the burden for those who were unsuccessful in their job searches.

Only a few had the privilege of a full year of study as I did; education was received year after year in summer school programs. Those who left before completing a college degree were handicapped in their search for a job. No consideration was given to their abundance of teaching experience. In the early and mid-1900s it was common for young women to teach without a degree. In the 1970s, however, quantitative years of teaching experience didn't outweigh the strength of a diploma.

There were those who did not recover from living on the edge of poverty. Today they are among the senior citizens who live off a meager social security or small pensions garnered from work in the years after leaving religious life. Neither the community nor pastors paid into social security during most of our teaching years. Not until

1971, when the U.S. Congress allowed social security payments to sisters, did the community begin paying into and receiving social security checks for the sisters. Most of us had left by that time.

One of my favorite teachers at the Academy worked as a secretary in a doctor's office in Chicago when she left. He had helped her build a retirement nest egg. When she moved from the city, she tried teaching religion again, but times and students had changed so much she couldn't cope. Due to bad management by one she trusted, her substantial retirement fund was lost. She now lives in a senior retirement home on Medicaid and has lost her sight. It is pitiful to see how some have struggled to exist after years and years of selfless dedication to the Church. There are no Sunday collections for their retirement.

Though nuns were the pioneers—the backbone of Catholic education and the founders of hospitals nationwide—there was no structure to assist them as they left. Former nuns have continued their service to the church, disappearing anonymously into the secular world, by choice, yes, but without a word of thanks or recognition for their contribution to Catholic institutions before or after they left. In fact, as a group, ex-nuns are often blamed for the demise of Catholic education. It took some time for the church to wake up, but eventually articles and books were written asking, *where did all the nuns go?* You may not recognize them as former nuns, but they are your neighbors, your children's teachers, nurses, social workers, lawyers, judges, civic officers, and community volunteers.

I was in limbo the summer I waited for my dispensation to be granted. I was neither a nun, nor an ex-nun. The last visit to Nauvoo to "sign out" was emotional.

"I have to ask you for your ring," Mother Clarisse said in a timid voice, her shoulders shrinking as though the emotional weight of these repeated scenes had diminished her strength. I fingered the shiny, gold ring inscribed in black with IHS, the symbol of my vows to Christ. The ring I wore carried a dedication to the centuries old Benedictine way of life. I turned it round and round coaxing it forward over my swollen knuckle—swollen from the days of playing basketball in the Academy gym. She clutched my hand in hers as I handed it to her. I felt her reluctance as she took it back, looking at me with watery eyes. We exchanged a warm farewell embrace. Never again would I have such a caring mentor in my life. The finality of the moment left me to face the future I had chosen. The sealed, brown envelope containing my dispensation paper from Rome arrived in the mail three weeks later. I was officially an ex-nun.

It was preferred that we didn't make a dramatic scene of saying our goodbyes up and down the halls from one department to another. A quiet exit was the norm.

Sister Sheila walked with me to the car that would take me away from Nauvoo for the last time. I was no longer a member of the community I had lived with and loved for twenty years. We cried together. I felt like a traitor. We shared a goodbye hug. I left her standing on the shaded sidewalk in front of the beige, brick dorm where I had walked down the hall and dropped my past into the incinerator. Her eyes were red. Once again, I had abandoned a best friend in pursuit of my own journey. I felt both guilt and selfishness.

I sat in the back of the convent car as another sister drove us back to the Moline mission house where I would continue to live, working temporarily at Alleman in the registrar's office. Sisters in the house would attend summer school at St. Ambrose. There was sadness in my heart and tears in my eyes. The sunny, cloudless morning did not reflect my dreariness. Sad though I was, I knew I didn't have time to wallow in guilt and self-pity. A job and a place to live loomed large on my agenda.

Chapter Twenty-Three – *Transition*

*I*n the summer of 1973, twenty years after leaving home for the convent, I was preparing for a life on my own for the first time.

The priests and brothers at the Rock Island school couldn't have been more supportive. Father Bob, the principal, volunteered to research openings in schools within their organization. He became my job-placement resource, and my financial safety net. Knowing I would need income until I got on my feet, he employed me for the summer as an assistant to Jean in the school registrar's office. Jean was my moral support during the first months of transition while I was getting used to who I was again. The thrill of depositing my first paycheck as Mary Ann Cahill into my first ever, checking account is still vivid. Following that, I applied for a credit card and got it with no trouble.

I was allowed to continue living at the parish mission house while I worked at the school through the summer. Father Bob, true to his word, found two positions open in schools administered by the Clerics of St. Viator. The momentum toward a new future was building.

A school in Kankakee, Illinois needed a typing teacher. In Arlington Heights, northwest of Chicago, there was a new opening for an office position in the high school academic offices. I called the principal at Kankakee and did a phone interview. Next, I borrowed my mother's car and went to Arlington Heights to meet with Brother Donald, the academic principal, to interview for the position of administrative assistant in the all-boys high school. The assistant office position was attractive in many ways—primarily because I would not be teaching. The challenge at hand was to help Brother Donald set up their first computer-scheduled classes. The summer job at Alleman would serve as an apprenticeship for the task. The only drawback to the position was the salary. He didn't know what it would be.

New to driving in the tangled spaghetti of interstates in and around Chicago, I found my way to Oakton Street in Arlington Heights. Debating on what dress to wear, something professional, but cheery and not nun-like, I chose a new, yellow dress with a navy and yellow plaid vest attached. My navy heels reverberated through the empty hallway announcing my arrival, as I searched for Brother Donald's office.

We got along famously in the interview. The job looked interesting to me. Eventually, the topic of salary came up.

"Are you saying that since this is a totally new position, there is no money in the budget for it? What does that mean in terms of salary?" I asked, stunned by the realization that I had made a trip to Chicago for a position that didn't exist.

"We didn't anticipate needing an extra person on staff, but I need help with the scheduling. We are computerizing our class schedules for the first time," said Brother Donald.

He promised he could get a salary into the budget and would be in touch to let me know the amount. I was pleased with the description of the job and everything about the school, but the prospects of an adequate salary looked dim to me.

"I'll wait to hear from you," I said picking up my purse to go.

Having worked with *no* salary for twenty years, the feel of money in my hand was not important. A roof over my head and food on the table were. Down state, Kankakee was looking better. At least there would be security. It would cost less to live there, and it was closer to my home. To a small-town, country girl, Chicago was daunting.

Brother Donald called within a week. He encouraged me to meet with him again for a second interview.

"The good news is that I got the President to agree to put your salary in the budget."

I was relieved.

"The questionable news is. . . ." He dropped his gaze, fidgeted with his pen, and mumbled the next words.

"The offer is seven thousand dollars," he said with a confident smile. He must have seen the look on my face. He quickly added, "With the promise of putting an increase in next year's budget," It was a pitiful amount, even for 1973.

My heart sank. I had many questions. Once the scheduling debacle was conquered, how would I know they would even need me the next year? What kind of increase could they promise? There were no definitive answers, only assurances that my position would be safe.

I had to think about whether I could live in Arlington Heights on that amount. I promised to get back to him after I thought it through.

I went to work putting pen to paper. After considering the cost of apartment rent, car, furniture, and clothes for work, I came up with a strangling budget. Seven thousand dollars was going to be a challenge, especially with an address in a Northwest Chicago suburb.

Weighing the pros and cons, considering the risk, contrasting rural Kankakee as a typing teacher with the excitement of living in the city and the challenge of administrative work, I decided to accept the position.

I sublet a one-bedroom apartment near the school. My survival success was going to take more than a stringent budget; it would take lots of prayer.

Before leaving Rock Island in July, I made my first big furniture purchases for my apartment—a sofa and a full-size mattress with box springs from Sears. Father John, a teacher friend at Alleman, gave me silverware and dishtowels his mother had given him for their house. Pat, another ex-nun friend from my Nauvoo community, who was working as a college professor in Davenport, Iowa, contributed a red plastic, mixing bowl to my "trousseau." All small things, but greatly appreciated. Nearly forty years later, the red plastic bowl is still my favorite mixing bowl. The dishtowels are threadbare, but still in the kitchen drawer and used often. They are symbols of my humble beginnings on the *outside*. My benefactors get a blessing with every use.

I had received a small inheritance from an aunt while I was in the community. According to community practices, monies given as an inheritance from family to members were put into an escrow account until the member either left or died. I remembered the money and requested it. It was enough to make deposits on a car and an apartment. Had it not been for my aunt's money, I would have left with no stipend or start-up goods, as others before and after me. When leaving the convent, we walked out the door with few possessions—a minimal wardrobe and personal items.

By 1973, when I left, I already had a few street clothes, but in conservative homemade styles. I had no jewelry or makeup. I wore only a touch of lipstick. I was a dead ringer for an ex-nun, a truth I was reluctant to volunteer.

My brother Joe came to Rock Island in July with his truck to help me move. He and Father John loaded my sofa, mattress, a few meager personal possessions, including my much-traveled high school trunk, and an old kitchen table my mother contributed to the cause. Joe and I headed to Arlington Heights. I was looking forward to setting up my own space in a new apartment.

Joe led the way; I followed in my first car—a little Toyota. Somewhere on Interstate 80, I saw a cushion from my new sofa fly off the back of the truck. I pulled over to pick it up. Before I could get to it, a rickety car zoomed by, a passenger jumped out, grabbed my cushion, and took off. Spontaneously, I speeded up to follow. I couldn't afford to lose a single cushion. I waved at Joe as I flew by in pursuit without a thought as to how I would get the cushion back or what kind of confrontation I might have on the highway. They pulled off at an exit heading off my route and I thought it best not to follow.

"What the heck were you doing?" Joe asked when we stopped to eat. He shook his head at my explanation. I think he feared for me being on my own in the world.

I left behind good memories of the two years spent in the experimental house in Moline/Rock Island. Among the good memories was my decorating handiwork in the basement recreation room where we gathered before Compline, our night prayers.

That room was perhaps a symbol of the creative life ahead of me. Somewhere inside there was a decorator waiting to escape.

The empty Arlington Heights apartment awaited my decorating talents. The door to Brandenberry Apartment 202 opened directly into the living room. A sliding glass door and small balcony were a few feet away.

"A balcony, how perfect could it get?" I said, describing it to my mother. It overlooked the parking lot. I was easily impressed.

It took just minutes to unload the truck. My first purchase in Arlington Heights was four plain maple chairs from Sears to go with my mother's old drop-leaf table. Though small and sparsely furnished, my new space felt like a palace, more shabby than chic. The miniscule kitchen had blue patchwork wallpaper on one wall—actually, there was *only* one wall. The dining area off the kitchen was just large enough for the table and two of the new maple chairs.

The Sears sofa—complete with new cushion replacement—sat against the long living room wall. Two of the versatile, maple chairs flanked it. I painted my high school trunk white and put it into service again, this time as a coffee table. The new mattress and frame filled the bedroom. A lone lamp sat on the floor.

Sears had dibs on much of my first paycheck. The little money left in my new bank account had to be stretched. I dug deep for every ounce of creativity in me to make my new space livable.

The sparse, but wonderful, little apartment was a symbol of my freedom. I walked around the three rooms feeling euphoric. Saturdays were free; I could sleep until noon, eat when I wanted, not get dressed until afternoon, or walk around naked if I wanted.

I didn't know what was ahead, but it would be all of my making, my decisions, my choices, and my responsibilities. God had led me this far; I trusted him to be with me now. I was thirty-seven years old and ready to live a new life.

Sister Sheila came to spend a weekend with me soon after I moved into the apartment. We shopped at Walmart for housekeeping essentials. I needed everything but could afford only essentials. Mother, Bill, and Lois were my first family guests. Pitying my minimal furnishings, Mother brought me a mirror and two end tables, which gave the living room a touch of normalcy.

Apartment dwellers are almost reclusive, for which I was grateful. I hadn't worked out a script to answer questions on my background yet. I wondered if I wasn't already under suspicion by the leasing staff, looking like a transient with next to no furniture. If they were curious, they didn't pry, but they must have speculated as to how a mid-thirties single woman could explain moving into an apartment with few clothes and not even a cup and saucer? I avoided inquisitive expressions with lips poised to ask questions.

Ever the social one and great communicator, I planned an Open House for former nuns from our Nauvoo community living in the vicinity. I needed the camaraderie and moral support of people like me. There must have been a half dozen of us within a thirty-minute drive.

"Wow, you've done a lot with next to nothing," Ann said. "When I started out, I used bricks and boards to make a bookcase."

They shared stories of their stringent beginnings. My limited culinary skills produced chips served in the red plastic bowl from Davenport, snacks, and cheese spread. We toasted with wine served in a mixture of containers, including barrel-shaped Chicago Bears glasses.

Taking pity on me, or just tired of sitting on the floor, Jean offered, "I have two chairs I don't use anymore. You're welcome to them, though they need repair."

Brother Donald's talents extended to creative carpentry with a designer's touch. He fixed the broken back slats of the wood-framed cushioned chairs. Those chairs stayed with me for eighteen years. The reupholstered seat cushions went from gold velvet to blue striped to floral peach.

A phone call now and then to Colorado kept me in regular communication with my friends Joan Cook and Sean. On a trip to Denver for Sean's wedding in the fall of '74, Joan gave me the book, *Out on a Limb*, by Shirley MacLaine. I was intrigued by MacLaine's experiences with past lives and her pursuit of meditation practices.

Though I wasn't in search of any past lives—I had enough to deal with in this life—her book did get me started on the path of reading more about meditation, growth in spirituality, and the metaphysical. I had a thirst for deepening my relationship with God. Since I never conquered the art of meditation in the convent, even after twenty years, I searched for anything that would give me the "how to" that

I had missed. I started reading Wayne Dyer, Deepak Chopra, Roy Eugene Davis, Paramahansa Yogananda's *Autobiography of a Yogi*, the Dalai Lama, and others. I needed to know how to set aside mental and physical distractions, clear space in my heart, and make room for God in meditation. I studied the chakras and experienced an alignment of my body that took me closer to a meditative state.

Two of my friends, Rosie and Barb, who had entered the community about the same time I did, lived in the area. They introduced me to a woman who led meditations. I will never forget the first time I experienced that totally relaxed feeling. It was as though my body was numb, and my mind was lifted up to the top of my head and beyond. I sat slouched in a straight, but comfortable chair, with my legs crossed as we chatted. I casually held a cup of coffee in one hand. The leader began the meditation with soft music; her words led us into the meditative state. My body began to straighten up of its own accord, my spine involuntarily corrected, bringing me out of my casual, slouched posture. My chin lifted, aligning my body. I found it necessary to set the coffee cup down or drop it. I could no longer hold it. My jaw relaxed, all mind distractions disappeared. After twenty minutes, the leader brought us out of the meditation. That was the first time I had ever gotten close to shutting out the constant distractions of my mind's ramblings. I was drawn closer to a place where God could find a way into my soul, and be heard. It seemed like real meditation, unlike anything I had experienced in the morning meditations in the convent chapel.

Barb, Rosie, and I, a trio of soul searchers, continued to meet, searching to improve our meditation practices. I had no awareness of Abbott Thomas Keating's method of Centering Prayer at that time. Neither did the convent community, as far as I knew. As Benedictines, we were part of a contemplative heritage, and yet did not seem to understand contemplation. At least I didn't. I often think what mountains could have been moved by the energy and contemplative efforts of that body of women sitting before God every morning meditating in unison. Though mountains may have been moved by the prayers of the group, I was sure I had not contributed.

My convent experience had been thirty minutes of meditation every day following Mass. As a community, we settled into our cushioned, blue stall seats to meditate reading a spiritual book. Instead of clearing my mind and making room for God, I was polluting it with thinking—often distracted thinking. After chanting the Divine Office of psalms, then Mass, the half-hour meditation practice sometimes became naptime for me, as well as others.

With a few hand-me-down furnishings from friends and family, I survived the first year on my salary. I could do nothing extra— no movies, eating out or unnecessary purchases. That didn't bother me; I wasn't used to an extravagant lifestyle. My social life consisted of attending athletic competitions at the school, staff parties, and gatherings of my ex-nun friends.

My economic status improved the second year. Brother Donald begged the president for my salary increase, as promised. Over time, I took over the class scheduling responsibility, matching teachers, students, and courses. I was becoming a permanent fixture on the staff; feeling secure in my job. After a few years, I was promoted to Assistant Principal, in charge of curriculum, and student registrations. That gave me the distinction of being the first and only woman administrator in all the schools staffed by Viatorians from Illinois to Las Vegas. Life was beginning to be good; the security of a good job with good people in a Catholic environment was a blessing— more blessings than many sisters found when leaving. The staff and faculty at the Viatorian school was a perfect community for me. The administrative staff knew I was an ex-nun; I didn't have to worry about tripping over my tongue and giving away the secret. They understood when big gaps in my social history were exposed.

I was one of the lucky ones. Many former nuns did not have the good fortune of finding a job in teaching. Teaching positions were especially scarce for religion teachers.

Many sisters left before they had completed degrees, though they had been teaching for years. They struggled to attend night classes while working as store clerks, waitresses, or in clerical jobs. One friend lived in a studio apartment in a low-rent district of Chicago while she attended school to finish her degree. She had a Murphy bed and a hotplate for cooking. It was an experience unlike the comforts of the convent.

"While the accommodations were the pits, I remember feeling euphoric...so independent and free." I knew exactly what she meant. Since the convent did not give us any monetary help or goods to get started, challenges were met through the kindness of friends, and when possible, donations from families. The vow of poverty in the convent was never felt in the same way; food, clothing, housing and medical support were never wanting. As nuns, we had no concerns for basic survival. As ex-nuns, we had to learn to survive.

I was one of thousands of women from convents across the country who took the same plunge; we left our vows and our convents. Whatever the reasons for leaving our religious community, many of the women pursued the good works that brought them to religious life in the beginning. They went into inner cities to do social work; they worked on Indian reservations as advocates for the disadvantaged. They married, became stepmothers and mothers. A grandmother in her sixties founded a school in Africa. One became a judge; another held a government position in a major city. Some continued in nursing and working with the terminally ill. Following the teaching profession, they became principals and received doctorates. Rosie, my meditation partner, pursued her long stifled talent for art. She shared her gift teaching around the world. Those who left were intelligent women who felt they could do God's work and make a contribution to society on the outside.

Collectively, the women who left during the late 1960s and 1970s were some of the most promising for the future of their religious communities. They were mature, intelligent, creative, and hardworking—all searching for ways to fulfill the Gospel in their lives without the constraints of community rules. One by one, they left and took their talents with them.

In a mini reunion of three friends—all ex-nuns, I met the husband of one of them. In the conversation, this down-to-earth, and extremely learned man often repeated the refrain, "Why did they let you women go?" It didn't make sense to him. It wasn't that they *let* us go. We were part of a movement in the Church to reach out beyond our convent walls. The departures left a gap in the community, a void never filled.

Vatican II may have been the catalyst that caused the grand exodus from convents between 1965 and 1980, but many of these women had struggled with a desire to leave years before. The message from well-meaning superiors or priest counselors was, "It is only natural to question your vocation in the beginning. It is a temptation from the Devil." Some young women came to the convent only because a priest told them they should be a nun. It took many years to muster the courage to leave. Some left without the blessing of a dispensation. Some *never* left.

At least one nun more than sixty years old wrote a letter to a younger sister who had left, expressing her admiration for the ex-nun. She applauded her for having the courage to leave in her mid-thirties. The elderly nun confessed her desire to leave the convent many years before, but no one was leaving, and she lacked the courage. Her life became increasingly bitter. It showed on her face. One has to wonder how that served God.

Chapter Twenty-Four –
Third Commitment

W ith convent days behind me, I was in no hurry to discover how the dating protocol had changed since 1953. I must confess I left no trail of broken hearts when I entered the convent after high school. Summers were short, vacations home were limited, and boarding school wasn't the ideal environment to entertain boys. Off-campus dating was not allowed. The boys I had dated from home were not Catholic. I could only imagine how they would have been spooked by the eyes of nuns around every corner, so I never invited them to any weekend events.

Junior and senior proms were held in the small, third floor gym, transformed with crepe paper, soft lights, and the requisite disco ball. Only as seniors could we leave campus for an after-prom picnic on Sunday. Bement was too distant to ask anyone to drive up for a heavily chaperoned visit, so I resorted to blind dates, arranged by classmates who lived closer to school. Asking a local Nauvoo boy would have only caused the nuns to watch us more closely, lest we try to meet secretly in town. None of the local boys seemed particularly interested in me anyway so I chose not to risk it. Some girls did take the risk, dated, and married after high school.

Sister Rita, Villa residence prefect and surrogate mother, met each prom date as they called for us. Corsages were pinned, pictures taken, and we walked across the street to the dance in the school auditorium.

After a few hours of dancing, in the crepe-papered auditorium with a disco ball transforming the barren gym into a dreamy evening, we'd walk back to the Villa residence with our dates. Each couple found a spot in the shadowed shrubbery of the building for a few private and intimate moments. If we lingered too long, Sister Rita would blink the porch lights to signal curfew. I still can't imagine how the boys felt this interlude was worth the money they spent on a suit and a corsage.

I never left the convent to fulfill any longing to be married or have a family. Dating after twenty years was not a high priority. Adjusting to my new life was challenge enough in the first couple of years. Some of my new friends, though, felt obligated to encourage me to explore the dating scene.

A co-worker on the St. Viator staff wanted to introduce me to her brother, Steve. Still not ready or interested in dating, I stalled for a while. Eventually, I agreed to go out to dinner with him.

My habit of using the term "okay" can be confusing to people; it can even send a wrong signal. It *is* unorthodox, I suppose. For example, I'd say, "Okay," I'm going to the next task" or "Okay, I'm finished with that one."

It was, however, confusing to a blind date after a quick kiss at the door when I said, "Okay." It wasn't enough to clarify my meaning— *okay, that's all for tonight.*

"Thank you for the nice evening and dinner." I politely said to this bear of a man who leaned in for another kiss.

"Okay, okay!" I said. He began pushing his luck with more kisses.

When I said, "okay, okay," it was not an invitation, it did not mean, come in, let's pursue this. It meant *okay, STOP. Why is that not clear?*

I contemplated kicking him in the shins to punctuate the meaning of "okay."

Another date with a casual acquaintance turned out harmless, but might have been dangerous in my naiveté. Jack lived in the same apartment building. He invited me out for a Friday evening, get-acquainted drink. Afterwards I invited him into my apartment for coffee and a chat. At thirty-seven years old, how does one account for ignorance of social topics, such as recent current events, movies, TV, and music of the 1960s? I was not ready to volunteer to a stranger that I had been under convent wraps for the last twenty years and had seen no movies or TV, had only listened to current music in the girls' dorm, and read no newspapers. That could cause an instant freak-out.

First, I had to deal with the awkward get-acquainted questions.

"Where did you move from?"

"Rock Island." That was easy.

"What did you do there?"

"I taught in a high school."

"How long were you there?" I felt we might be getting into dangerous territory. To say two years would only prompt, "What did you do before that?" I thought it best to detour the questions to focus on his interests.

He asked if I knew about REMs. I had no clue.

"What does REM stand for?"

He explained that it stood for rapid eye movements, something he was studying. "Movements of the eyelids can be counted when the eyes are closed." I wasn't sure what that would reveal, but I acted interested.

"Close your eyes and I will count your REMs." I closed them while he counted. Sensing this might not be a wise exercise with a virtual stranger, I quickly tired of the experiment. He was perfectly harmless, but in my naiveté how could I be sure? It was a short date, but long enough for me to know I could begin dating on my own, without the safety net of friends finding me a date.

I first saw Hal at The Raggedy Ann. My sister-in-law, Lois, Bill's wife, owned the Raggedy Ann restaurant on Bodman Street in Bement. Lois was known as the best cook in town; she drew a repeat crowd. When I was home for a visit with my mother, Lois suggested we come by the restaurant for lunch. It was a set up. At the counter sat Hal, the local gas station owner, having lunch. He was a regular, especially fond of her homemade pie. He kept turning from his counter stool, stealing glances in our direction. Lois was behind this *accidental* encounter. She admitted telling him I was out of the convent and available.

"Would you go out with him if he called?" she asked.

"Maybe he should call if he wants to find out." I didn't know the answer to that myself, but I didn't want to communicate through my sister-in-law. Regardless, I needed time to think about my answer if he did call.

Though he was well-known to my family, who traded at his gas station, I only vaguely remembered him as the manager on the high school football team. I didn't expect him to call, and it didn't matter to me. Dating was not high on my to-do list.

Opportunities for social activities were plentiful, thanks to my friends on the staff at St. Viator. They included me in frequent social gatherings.

"How would you like to take a whitewater rafting trip down the Colorado River?" Gerry, the registrar at St. Viator, asked. Without hesitation, I agreed. Four of us gals, Gerry, her sister, another friend and I, flew to Colorado where we met up with the rafting company. With our minimal gear in tow—a sleeping bag, sun lotion, and camera—the rafting crew delivered us to a quiet little stream. We wore swimsuits under shirts and cutoffs. Climbing into one of three, six-by-twelve foot rubber rafts with a half-dozen other adventurers, we launched off toward the Colorado River for a three-day and two-night camping experience.

Growing up in flat, Illinois farm country, I found the Colorado River and mountain views spectacular. After hours on the river, some of us jumped into the water and floated along side the raft to cool our sun-baked skin. The calm surface water was deceiving, the current was swift. Soon our guide signaled to the guides in the following rafts by pointing ahead down river. Gradually, the stillness was broken by the distant sound of tumbling water. Novices at rafting, we didn't recognize the first sounds of rapids. The tempo of the rushing water increased to a roar. There was no doubt we would soon see whitewater splashing on rocks.

"Back in the raft!" the guides ordered. "Cover your cameras and secure your gear!"

Nervous and excited, we anticipated the whitewater ride we had signed on for. Around every bend of the river, the smashing of waves grew louder and closer, until finally, the raft was riding the crests and depths of the rapids. Our experienced guides battled the waves, saving the rafts from crashing into boulders. No sooner would we catch a breath, than another rush of waves pounded the raft, splashing water over us. It was both scary and exhilarating.

Relief came when we reached the overnight campsite. Sleeping under the stars, cooking bacon and eggs at the edge of the river, and surviving the whitewater rapids of the Colorado, still tops the list of my best-ever vacations. The magnificent scenery as we floated deep at the base of the black rock canyon walls was awe inspiring. No denying God's majestic artwork.

A few weeks after my lunch at The Raggedy Ann, Hal called me to ask for a date. "I didn't really expect that you would accept," he told me later. "I was divorced and not a Catholic, you were a Catholic ex-nun. What were the chances?"

For those same reasons, I felt it would be harmless to accept a date with him. Nothing would come of it. I wasn't interested in a relationship, especially not with someone from my hometown. Bement was far away, and I had no thoughts of moving back there. On the other hand, I hadn't dated much yet, so it was a chance to go out with someone safe from my hometown. And if he wanted to make the 150-mile trip to Arlington Heights for a single Saturday night date, then I was game.

The first Saturday in June was a deliberate choice. I knew I would be unavailable on the following Sunday because it was graduation day at St. Viator, and I was scheduled to announce the two hundred graduate names as they received their diplomas. As a rookie—the only woman on the administrative team—I drew the announcing duty. It was presented to me as an honor to be selected. I knew better. The men were relieved to escape the challenge of wrapping a tongue around all those Polish, Italian, and Scandinavian names. I was up to the task after years of teaching in schools with Olzewskis, Scacciferros, and Wasilewskis.

The ceremony gave me a legitimate reason not to prolong the first date into Sunday. If it worked out, there could be other weekends. If it didn't, we'd both be saved the agony of another awkward day spent together. I suffered a twinge of guilt, since he gave up a day's work to drive three hours for a date that would last only a few hours, including dinner.

From my apartment window, I could see him coming up the sidewalk. He wore khaki slacks, a light blue, short-sleeved, collared shirt, and brown loafers, his hair a fresh crew cut. A muscular chest and arms were evident through the crisp shirt. He checked his watch; I checked the kitchen clock; it was on the threshold of 4 pm. He was prompt.

My apartment was less than a five-minute elevator ride to the second floor. I stared at the door. No knock. *He couldn't have gotten lost. Did he have second thoughts?* There was no reason to be nervous, but I was. The knock was firm. I stalled a minute before answering, glancing at my image in the mirror. After five changes, the simple, light blue shift looked right, not too fussy, kind of dressy casual.

"Hi! Welcome to Arlington Heights. Any trouble finding me?"

He lied. "No, your directions were good." He confessed later that he had been totally lost for more than an hour on the angled streets with names that change from one suburb to another. The fact that he was still on time, told me he had built in getting-lost time. He was either a good planner or insecure, or maybe both.

Proud of my new digs, I gave him a quick tour around my sparsely furnished apartment—all three rooms. The tour consisted of a single-file walk through the galley kitchen, into the dining room, which connected to the living room. Lastly, I gave him a peek into room three, the bedroom, exposing the mattress on the floor. I blushed at showing him the bedroom, but without it, there was hardly a reason to pretend it was a tour. The apartment wasn't really impressive to anyone who owned a home, as he did, but it was all mine, put together piece-by-recycled piece. I offered him a glass of wine. He looked a little surprised. I suspected he didn't think an ex-nun would have wine available. After a bit of idle chatter, I suggested we go to dinner.

The newness of his car's comfortable, white leather seats filled my senses with memories of home—new cars were big events in our family. I slipped in as he held the door.

"Love your car. New?"

"A couple of months," he said. I could sense a pride in his powder blue, Mercury Cougar LX. No doubt, I scored points admiring his new ride.

He looked uncomfortable settling into the booth at the nice restaurant, his confidence wavering in that setting. I guessed he was more at home sitting at the counter in the Raggedy Ann Diner where the menu was basic and familiar. Dinner was nice, conversation good.

We both relaxed, sharing mutually familiar topics from our earlier hometown days. He seemed continually surprised that I knew the same people he did. I had not been around for years, but I did grow up there, and everybody knows everybody in a small town. He seldom took his eyes off me through dinner. I fidgeted with the silver, avoiding his gaze. It was a casual dinner date with no future expectations, at least not on my part. In the last two years, my vision had never extended beyond day-to-day survival, so I was taken aback when his questions kept returning to my future plans. I had no long-range plans. I dodged the inquiry.

Back at the apartment, warmed by how well the evening went, we relaxed with a cup of coffee. He drank his black, so did I. Insignificant trivia, but one of those early minor details that suggest compatibility. I couldn't help but notice he was more handsome than I remembered.

Balancing the cup on his knee, he continued focusing those Paul Newman blue eyes on me as he leaned forward and inquired, "So, what *are* your plans? Do you see yourself getting married in the near future?

Married? My thoughts ran crazy. *Was he kidding?* The evening had gone well, but not *that* well. Then it crossed my mind. *Maybe he doesn't plan to make another 150-mile trip to the suburbs of Chicago unless there is a future in it.* Knowing he was not long divorced, I couldn't imagine he had immediate, serious-relationship plans either.

"Married?" I choked, rescuing my cup from a near drop. Marriage was nowhere in my vision. Freedom was still a fresh experience.

"I've only been free a few months, you know. Another commitment? So soon? I don't think so."

"But surely you think about it, don't you?" Maybe it was my imagination, but I felt pressed beyond my comfort level. It was as though a next dinner might depend on my answer.

Not to be coerced, and since we were just casual friends at this point, I responded casually, though I stumbled for words, "Well, no, and if, and when, I do think about it, ah, I guess since I live in the city now, ah, it will probably be a guy from up here."

"Like what kind of guy?"

I stuttered as I searched for a further description of a perfect mate. "I dunno—I hadn't thought about it. I suppose someone professional, who likes classical music, dinners out, theatre, an interest in nature, and all sports."

Off the top of my head, I felt that summed up a daunting if unrealistic, applicant resume. The subject was dropped. The description didn't fit him at all, and we both knew it.

The next day, lined up for the graduation ceremony, the "Pomp and Circumstance" interrupted the mental replaying of our Saturday night dinner date. Except for the pressure about my future plans, the evening had gone better than I expected. Lois didn't call for a report on the date. She probably got one from him at Monday's lunch counter. I thought my mother would probably not want to know details, so I spared her that conversation.

Living alone and managing my own life with the freedom to do and go as I pleased was still intoxicating for me. Marriage wasn't in my plans.

My investment knowledge started gnawing at me. Throwing money away on rent seemed irresponsible. I knew little of the expenses of home ownership, but I thought I could swing a down payment and mortgage on a townhouse. With virtually no income track record at thirty-eight, I was not a good risk for a mortgage company. Just being a woman was a strike against me. It helped that I had lived conservatively; I managed to convince them of my steadfastness and earning potential. Brother Donald vouched for my stable career path. I gave little thought to how I would make mortgage payments if my job ended.

Loyal big brother Joe came up to scope out the townhouse I had in mind to buy. His real mission, I suspect, was to make a report to my mother on my mental state. My brother Dick advised me to keep renting, "You might want to move to Florida someday." I couldn't see how one would exclude the other.

It took two weeks, but Hal called again. Admittedly, I would have been disappointed if he hadn't.

"I thought you'd never call," a sure give away.

"Wow. I wasn't sure if I should." He was obviously pleased with my eagerness to hear from him. Whatever my flawed logic, I agreed to another date. And so this handsome, blue-eyed, hometown guy, with country music roots, a mechanic's background, and a singular interest in Cubs baseball, was willing to drive many miles out of his comfort zone to take me to dinner again and again.

No denying I was flattered by his attention, but it still didn't change my goals. A serious relationship was not in my plans, and certainly not marriage. I was just beginning to establish my new life. Simply answering to my family name once again took getting used to. Until now, in all of my adult life, I had not been addressed as Miss Cahill. Almost forty years old and a few years out of the convent, I was experiencing a new beginning. I felt seventeen again, ready to launch my life. Free to make my own decisions, whether major or minor, right or wrong.

Three of my friends from St. Viator—all husbands of women I worked with—offered to help me move to the new townhouse I bought. We needed a truck. I called on Hal to see if he would consider coming up to help me move. My friends would meet my secret suitor for the first time. I felt introducing him to my close friends would be tantamount to taking him home to meet the family, suggesting I was serious about this guy. And I couldn't be—hometown guy, divorced, and all that. I sensed asking him to help me move was an encouraging sign to him. His take-care-of-me actions suggested he was *the* guy in my life.

Decorating the new townhouse absorbed all my free time. The gold-striped Sears sofa became the centerpiece of my decorating scheme. New expenses related to owning a home kept my creativity in check. I recycled the old church pew Sister Martha had given me. Once a blue-and-white kitchen bench in the apartment, it became a sophisticated entry bench in black and gold. After multiple color changes, indoor and outdoor use, it gave up the ghost years later. It was the last physical evidence of my convent days, except for my high school trunk that served as a coffee table for a couple of years until Mom took pity on my minimalist decorating and parted with one of her old coffee tables.

As I started life over on half a shoestring, I found creativity and frugality to be my constant resources. The promise of a life of poverty in the convent had taught me to be frugal with God's gifts and detached from material things. Benedict wrote . . . *no one may presume to . . . retain anything as his own, nothing at all . . . not a single item.* (Rule, Ch. 33.) With that kind of training, I was inspired to find multiple uses for ordinary things. I recycled before it was popular.

With the security of a job and now the added responsibility of living under my own roof, I developed a confidence that I could handle whatever was to come. Though naïve, I had a positive attitude about my unknown future. I was blessed with an inner guidance, benefiting from *ask and you shall receive.* The townhouse wasn't much bigger than my one bedroom apartment—my furniture nearly filled it. The second bedroom of the townhouse remained empty. Future plans included a combination office/sitting room/guest room.

For privacy, I stapled a gold second-hand drapery to the wall above the living room window, newspaper covered the kitchen window. Drapery rods were a luxury beyond my means. It may have been primitive, but it was mine. I could grow into it. The mortgage took priority; I had to save my money before I could think of adding furniture or accessories. I was smart enough not to consider my credit card as an option.

Once again, I called on Hal to help me build a shelving unit for books in the second bedroom. He spent his weekend working on my project after putting in fifty hours during the week at his station. Was he getting more committed or was I? I wasn't sure. I didn't want to think about it. I had known him for several months by that time, and he was definitely a good friend. A further relationship still was not in my plans. Life held too many possibilities that I had yet to explore. New home ownership anchored me to Arlington Heights, removing any possibility of moving back to Bement in case that was in his mind.

I asked Hal to be my date for the St. Viator High School annual fundraising concert. Singer John Gary was the featured entertainer. The evening included dinner afterwards with my administrative colleagues. It was a dress-up affair for which I needed a long dress. Putting my sewing skills to work once again, I made a long, black dress with scoop neckline and bell sleeves. I wasn't sure if Hal would be comfortable at the fancy affair, or if he would like the singer, but he agreed to go, and surprised me with an orchid corsage. It was the first introduction of Hal to the rest of my friends and colleagues at the school.

As entertainers will do, John Gary came down to the audience, and sang a love song directly to me in the front row, catching me and Hal in the spotlight. The excitement of the beautiful evening carried us through dinner with friends, and back to the townhouse. Another glass of wine heated up the passion we were both feeling. Hal began to press for more of a commitment from me. I was weakening.

"I don't want to push, but when do you think you are going to admit that we have something serious here?" he asked.

"I love being with you, but I'm just not ready to have a permanent commitment. I'm still getting used to living on my own."

He accepted and understood, but wanted more.

We kept our dating quiet from the hometown crowd. I didn't want to be the catalyst for embellished gossip around our small town. The gossip would only embarrass him, if we broke up. He had to live there.

"Don't you hurt him," my mother admonished, knowing that I was not serious about getting married. Hal was her garage man in Bement. She counted on him to service her car. She liked him and trusted him, and didn't want me messing up her friendship with him or hurting him.

I remember the first time I was home for a weekend visit after we started dating. I watched for his car and quickly answered the door when he drove up. I had shopped for a special dress for the occasion. When he gasped a little as I opened the door, I knew the dark, forest green print dress with crisp white collar and cuffs was the perfect choice. It was the first time I had gone on a date from home since I was seventeen. He had only been to the house to pick up and deliver Mom's car. We both felt awkward. There was no kiss at the door. After a brief chat with my mother, we virtually sneaked out of town. Still keeping our growing relationship private, I felt like maybe I should duck down in the seat so as not to be seen. I moved closer to him as we drove to dinner at the Blue Mill restaurant in Decatur, his favorite. Once in the parking lot of the restaurant, I waited for him to come around and open the door for me.

"There's something I can't wait for any longer," he said.

"What?" I said as I turned back to him.

"This," he said as he reached over and gave me a serious kiss catching me off guard.

After dinner, we both longed for more of those tender kisses, but with no place to go, he pulled into a car dealer parking lot. The steamed windows gave us away. It was obvious his car was not one waiting to be sold. A policeman drove up beside us, knocked on the window, and suggested we move on. I'm sure he expected teenagers, but found two middle-aged kids with no home to go to. Laughing with embarrassment, we did just that, moved on.

The more trips he made to Arlington Heights, the more serious we became. He wanted a commitment from me; he was willing to sell his business and move if I would agree that I would marry him. He was tired of spending his weekend nights at the Holiday Inn. For him to even think of selling his successful business, and move to a strange city just to be with me was a magnanimous gesture of his love. It was more than I could ask of him just yet.

I knew marrying him would not be simple, not if I wanted to be married in the Catholic Church, and I did. I had no intention of giving up my religion. Anyway, it would have hurt my mother tremendously. For me to go from her little Hail Mary girl, to her nun daughter, to leaving the Church would break her heart.

I remember exactly the moment I knew I was going to say yes. We were in the townhouse on a Saturday night sharing personal thoughts and goals—a deeper conversation than usual. Touched by his openness and his patience, I began to cry. His gentle, sweet tenderness and sincerity struck me as the most beautiful and precious gift I might receive. I knew that he was someone who would love me and accept me for who I was, and who I might want to be.

"I'm ready to get married," I said. "I'm ready to marry you."

He was stunned. After his many months of pursuit, I'd caught him off guard.

When he comprehended what I'd said, he turned to look at me. "Do you mean it? Are you sure?" He moved to hold me in his arms, not letting go for the longest time, as if he were afraid I might change my mind.

For a Catholic to marry a divorced, non-Catholic and remain in the good graces of the Church, there were challenging requirements to be addressed. His previous marriage would need to be annulled. That was a terrible subject to bring up. As distasteful as that was to him, because he had two children, he was willing to do it. Neither of us knew what was involved or how long it would take.

To make the commitment official, we planned to announce it to our families with an engagement ring at Christmas. Hal was ready to begin the sale of his gas station business and home, and move to Arlington Heights. We were hoping that all things would come together for a wedding in July. It turned out that selling his gas station and moving to Arlington Heights were simple in comparison to navigating the required annulment and red tape to marry in the Church. If our love would last through the process, I knew we had something special.

I felt such guilt as he went through the process of a series of questionnaires, both personal and prying. He endured interviews with chancery priests, who somehow had the authority to say "yes" or "no" to us getting married. Once again, Church authority was controlling my life. Not only did Hal have to submit to humiliating questions about his previous marriage, but he also had to request his ex-wife to give testimony about their marriage. Understandably, the mother of his children resented that we were asking for their marriage to be annulled. Every step of the process proved his love even more. I believe jumping through all the required and humiliating hoops tainted his view of the Catholic Church. Before suffering the invasions of his privacy, he had gone to Mass with me on a regular basis.

He tolerated it because of my desire to be married with the sanction of my church. My faith had always been the foundation of my life; I couldn't turn my back on it. In retrospect, I have asked myself, *would I put him through this if it were today?* I don't think so.

By this time, no one was surprised to learn that we were engaged and making wedding plans. Hal sold his new house and his lucrative gas station business, which provided his only income at a time when he still had two kids to put through college. He was leaving behind his hometown, where he was a respected business man, leaving his parents, relatives, and his friends to move to a strange city, where he knew no one but my friends. He had no job. He was boldly courageous and blindly in love.

On a tight budget, he found a cheap, pay-by-the-week motel—or maybe even by-the-hour—near my townhouse. He spent only his sleeping hours at the motel. My young neighbor was appalled when she discovered that Hal was not living with me. She would have been more appalled if she'd seen the crusty motel. On the other hand, I don't doubt our families were equally appalled, believing he *was* living with me. His parents and my mother would have disapproved. Living together was not in our comfort zone, nor would it have been a good example for his children. We played down the motel where he was staying. It was cheap, but such a rat hole. He didn't even let his parents see it when they came up for the wedding. I was in it once. Pangs of guilt gripped me for making him spend months in that dark, dingy, one ceiling-light-bulb room. It was best that as little light as possible was shed on the place. We moved all of his clothes to my closet just before the wedding. When my mother took one look at the full closet including his clothes, it no doubt confirmed her worst fears—he *was* living with me. Maybe afraid of the answer, she never asked.

Hal searched for any job he could find related to his background with cars. He sold auto parts for one company, worked at a tire store for another, and ultimately bought a plum of a gas station on the busy corner of Route 12 and West Dundee Road in Palatine. He was back in business and loving it. I was his bookkeeper.

Annulment approval for confirming our wedding date was still pending. We had planned on July 24, my birthday, to be married. We held our breath that the annulment would be finalized and we could go ahead with our plans. It came through just in time.

Pending the annulment, we could not reserve a church for the date. We wanted it to be small, with as little expense as possible, so we chose to have the ceremony in my home. Priests were saying Masses in private homes at that time, though it was not common. Permission might not have been granted to perform a wedding Mass in a home if it involved lots of publicity. So as not to get the local St. Viator priests in the middle of a controversial situation, I asked Father John, my priest friend from Alleman High School in Rock Island, to officiate. Father Pat, from St. Viator, agreed to intercede for us in getting the wedding registered locally. I regret not having the courage to ask Brother Donald or Father Pat if we could be married in the magnificent chapel of the Viatorian headquarters in Arlington Heights. Seeing me walk down a church aisle with an organ resonating would have pleased my mother, I'm sure. Her last memory of me walking down an aisle was when I put on the long, black habit and covered my head with a white veil. I would have liked to substitute that memory for one of me in a white wedding dress in a beautiful chapel.

The wedding Mass ceremony in my small living room, with his family and mine, was sweet and simple. Yellow-centered daisies dressed the room, the coffee table donated by my mother served as the altar. My white wedding dress had a v-neckline and cape-like sleeves. I carried a basket overflowing with white daisies to complement the wreath of daisies and white baby's breath in my hair. Hal looked handsome in a black suit with a white, French-cuffed shirt and a gray, black and white striped tie. I could count on one hand the number of times he'd worn a long-sleeved shirt in our time together. Five out of the six times were to please me, the sixth to please his daughter at her wedding. Kim even got him into a tuxedo. Hal's children, Kent and Kim were teenagers. Kim still lived with her mother while Kent was in college in Decatur. I saw them infrequently, but we always got along when we were together. Hal and I agreed we would not have children. At forty-one, I felt too old to take on the role of mother, though I assured him I was happy that he had two. We could enjoy being grandparents in the future.

Kim helped me dress, then she on the recorded music and I walked into the living room to stand by Hal at the "altar." Kent and my niece, Janet, did the readings during the Mass. I'm sure it was strange for my family to participate in a home Mass, especially a home wedding Mass. It was no doubt even stranger for Hal's family. They were not Catholic and probably had never been to a Catholic wedding or even inside a Catholic Church.

We had reserved the Barn of Barrington Restaurant, Barrington, Illinois, for our reception. The rustic setting and weathered, barn-like building suited us perfectly. The guests arrived ahead of us and greeted us as we climbed the picturesque burgundy-carpeted staircase to a private dining room. Champagne and toasts preceded our sit-down dinner. The restaurant prepared an impressive, three-tiered cake topped with a mound of daisies. Wedding pictures captured the requisite cake cutting, but no smashing of cake in our faces. Back at the town house, we changed into travel clothes, and headed off on our honeymoon to Lake Geneva, Wisconsin.

Our married life together grew better with each day. We rode through the ups and downs with little to no drama. We were at peace with one another as we adjusted to each other's idiosyncrasies. He was neat, I was not. Whenever we had a house for sale, it was his closet I instructed agents to show. I learned to cook basic, boring, meat-and-potato meals, his favorites, in lieu of trying gourmet recipes or even casseroles. He put up with my passion for current news. I became a Cubs fan and learned to love country music.

When comparing my two lives—in the convent and in marriage—I found the years of absorbing Benedict's Rule on relationships applicable to both. Benedict based his Rule on scripture. *They should each try to be the first to show respect to the other (Romans 12:10) supporting with the greatest patience one another's weakness of body or behavior, and earnestly competing in obedience to one another. No one is to pursue what is judged better for self, but instead what is judged better for someone else. (Rule, Ch. 72)*

I like to think that my years in the convent being a good nun had something to do with making me a good wife. Benedict's chapter on the tools of good works speaks to getting along with people—spouses are people.

... harbor neither hatred nor jealousy of anyone, and do nothing out of envy. Do not love quarreling; shun arrogance. If you have a dispute with someone, make peace ... before the sun goes down. (Rule, Ch. 4)

More than thirty years into our marriage, on one ordinary day, I stood at the kitchen stove preparing the obligatory meat and potatoes. Hal was relaxed in his favorite, black-leather recliner in the sitting room near the kitchen. I don't remember the topic of our conversation, but I'll never forget the moment. In a lull in the conversation, he said, "You changed my whole life."

"I did?" I looked up in amazement at his impromptu comment, totally out of context. Stunned, I couldn't think to ask *how*, or *why*, or say anything. The moment was wonderfully special. There were many times I heard "I love you," many admissions from him that I waited on him too much, but never anything so significant to me as "You changed my whole life."

"Yes," he said. And he went on watching the news as though he had asked "What's for dinner?"

For me, that simple, but grand, statement gave meaning to my life like nothing ever had.

It answered the question, why the killer tornado spared me at age seven—*to change a life.*

It explained my calling to the convent to become a giving and patient woman—*to change a life.*

Clearly, Sister Rose played a major role in bringing me to that moment—*to change a life.*

What could be more spiritual than changing a person's *whole* life? My soul must have planned our life together for that purpose. The combination of grace received, and intuition followed in my lifetime, led me on a continuing path of fulfilling that plan. As my life progressed, I grew closer to reaching the apex of the spirituality I had searched for, but never found, in the convent.

Afterword

As many times as I revisited the monastery for reunions and gatherings in the years after I left, I never received any answers to the longstanding questions I carried for years. The questions that drove me to doubt my place in that Benedictine community remained unanswered.

Why was it that no one stood up for the "naughty nine" at that fateful community meeting when my heart broke? Why did not one Sister even ask us for an explanation of the proposal in the days after the meeting? How did they seem to know the content of the proposal though it had not been distributed? The silence and those missing answers left me with only one conclusion at that time. After living with the sisters from the age of fourteen, they really didn't know me at all.

Thirty-seven years later, I got my answers. While writing this book, I visited friends at the Monastery and learned that Sister Rose had met secretly with a group of sisters, prior to that fateful community chapter meeting.

I was told that at that secret meeting she apprised them of the proposal and her opposition to it. They were sworn to secrecy about their meeting and understood that they were not to speak in favor of the proposal for change at the Academy, or in defense of those of us who signed it.

The reason behind the failure of our proposal to even be discussed had haunted me all these years. The revelation came as no surprise.

It confirmed the power behind the stonewalling—the source of the deafening silence in the room. I forgave Sister Rose long ago. Forgiveness relieved the pain and allowed me to move on. I am grateful to her for inadvertently opening the door that led me out of the convent and into a new and fulfilling life.

In subsequent years, school enrollment continued a gradual decline. Hail Mary Catholic country girls no longer came for the Catholic education or the adventure as I had. A few wealthy families from Mexico City sent their daughters to the school for a good education. Efforts were made to boost enrollment numbers with additional Mexican girls. The monastery subsidized the school for many years, but the proposal of years before would portend the eventual closing. The once thriving Academy, the lifeblood of the convent, eventually closed its doors in 1997. Our fears were realized. Not long after, St. Mary's Monastery also closed. The Mormons bought all properties. Having come full circle, they rebuilt their Temple, restoring the town to its original Mecca for Mormons.

The community of Benedictines left Nauvoo and rebuilt their convent in Rock Island, Illinois, but no longer staffed a school. Their move marked the third major migration from Nauvoo.

Sister Rose did not live to see the fateful events. Her heart would have been broken.

If ever I felt guilt for not keeping my vow of stability, I turned to Mother Ricarda's words in *Shades in the Fabric*, her commentary on those two Sisters who left the community in 1922.

Under the affliction of a deep wound—especially that of humiliation—one can "fall out of love" with the surroundings that caused it. –Shades in the Fabric

CPSIA information can be obtained at www.ICGtesting.com
Printed in the USA
LVOW11s2314300116

473024LV00001B/2/P